KU-297-844

Top 25
Amsterdam

TERESA FISHER

AA Publishing
Find out more about AA Publishing and the wide range
of travel publications and services the AA provides by
visiting our web site at *www.theAA.com/bookshop*

About this Book

ORGANIZATION

This guide is divided into six sections:
- Planning Ahead, Getting There
- Living Amsterdam—Amsterdam Now, Amsterdam Then, Time to Shop, Out and About, Walks, Amsterdam by Night
- Amsterdam's Top 25 Sights
- Amsterdam's Best—best of the rest
- Where to—detailed listings of restaurants, hotels, shops and nightlife
- Travel facts—practical information

In addition, easy-to-read side panels provide fascinating extra facts and snippets, highlights of places to visit and invaluable practical advice.

The colours of the tabs on the page corners match the colours of the triangles aligned with the chapter names on the contents page opposite.

Contents

Planning Ahead

WHEN TO GO

Most tourists visit Amsterdam between April and September; late March to late May is the time to see tulips in bloom. June brings the Holland Festival of art, dance, opera and theatre. Although winter can be cold and damp, December is crowded with Christmas shoppers and those staying for the festive season.

TIME

Amsterdam is one hour ahead of London, six hours ahead of New York and nine hours ahead of Los Angeles.

AVERAGE DAILY TEMPERATURE

	JAN	FEB	MAR	APR	MAY	JUN	JUL	AUG	SEP	OCT	NOV	DEC
°F	41°F	43°F	48°F	55°F	63°F	68°F	72°F	72°F	68°F	57°F	46°F	41°F
°C	5°C	6°C	9°C	13°C	17°C	20°C	22°C	22°C	20°C	14°C	8°C	5°C

Spring (March to May) is at its most delightful in May—with the least rainfall.
Summer (June to August) is the sunniest of the year but good weather is never guaranteed.
Autumn (September to November) gets wetter, although September is a popular time to visit. The weather is often chilly and drizzly as winter approaches.
Winter (December to February) can be cold, and temperatures can drop so low that the canals freeze. Strong winds can increase the chill factor, and fog can blot out the sunlight for days.

WHAT'S ON

February *Chinese New Year*: In Chinatown (around Zeedijk).
Carnival: Celebrated as a preamble to Lent.
March *Stille Omgang* (second Sun): Silent procession.
April *National Museum Weekend* (mid-month): Museums lower entrance fees.
Koninginnedag (30 Apr): The official Queens' birthday.
May *Remembrance Day* (4 May): Honours World War II victims.
Liberation Day (5 May):

Marking the end of the German Occupation in 1945.
National Windmill Day (second Sat).
National Cycling Day (second Sun).
June *Holland Festival*: International arts festival.
Grachetenloop canal race (second Sun): Along the banks of Prinsengracht and Vijzelgracht.
July *Summer Festival*: Alternative arts festival.
August *Prinsengrachtconcert* (last Fri): Classical music recitals on barges outside the Hotel Pulitzer.

September *Bloemencorso* (first Sat): Flower-laden floats from Aalsmeer to Amsterdam.
National Monument Day (second Sat): Usually closed monuments and buildings open.
Jordaan Folk Festival (second week): Music, street parties.
October *Antiques Fair* (last weekend): On Spiegelkwartier.
November *Sinterklaas* (Santa Claus) *Parade* (mid-Nov).
December *Pakjesavond* (5 Dec): Traditional day for present giving.
Oudejaarsavond (31 Dec): Street parties, fireworks.

AMSTERDAM ONLINE

www.channels.nl
Use this website to take a virtual walk around the city. Pick any street and the site will display photographs and links to hotels, museums, shops or restaurants on that street. The forum is full of useful hotel and restaurant reviews written by visitors to Amsterdam.

www.amsterdam-hotels.org
www.holland-hotels.com
Accommodation: The first site represents a cross-section of hotels in the city, from budget to deluxe, including apartments and houseboats. The second covers the whole of the Netherlands, and is useful if you want to travel further afield or find hotels in nearby towns when all the hotels in Amsterdam are full. Both sites have up-to-date details of tariffs, special offers and room availability, with pictures of typical rooms on offer and maps showing the precise location.

www.visitamsterdam.com
www.holland.com
Official tourist board sites: The first covers Amsterdam and the second the whole of the Netherlands. They are good for information about exhibitions, events and festivals. Both have online accommodation booking.

www.dinnersite.nl
Say what kind of food you like and you'll get a comprehensive list of Amsterdam restaurants to suit. Over 9,000 restaurants are featured on this site, covering all parts of the Netherlands, and you can specify criteria such as 'child friendly', 'smoke free', or 'wheelchair accessible'. You can also use the site to make reservations online.

www.bmz.amsterdam.nl
For everything you could ever want to know about the architecture in Amsterdam, visit this excellent and informative site belonging to Amsterdam Heritage.

PRIME TRAVEL SITES

www.eurostar.com
For details of international rail services.

www.ns.nl
Journey planner for getting around Holland by train.

www.hollandsepot.dordt.nl
Fascinating information (mostly in Dutch) on traditional Dutch food, with recipes.

www.fodors.com
A complete travel-planning site. You can research prices and weather; book air tickets, cars and rooms; pose questions (and get answers) to fellow travellers; and find links to other sites.

CYBERCAFÉS

EasyInternetcafé
✉ Reguliersbreestraat 22 and at Damrak 33;
www.easyeverything.com
🕐 Daily 7.30–11.30

Freeworld Internet Café
✉ Kort Nieuwendijk 30;
www.freeworld-internetcafe.nl 🕐 Daily 10am–midnight

Lost in Amsterdam
✉ Nieuwendijk 19; www.lostinamsterdam.com
🕐 Daily 10am–midnight

Getting There

VISAS AND TRAVEL INSURANCE

Visas are not required for EU, US or Canadian nationals, but you will need a valid passport. EU citizens can obtain health care with the production of form E111. However, insurance to cover illness and theft is strongly advised.

MONEY

The euro (€) is the official currency of the Netherlands. Banknotes are in denominations of 5, 10, 20, 50, 100, 200 and 500 euros; and coins are in denominations of 1, 2, 5, 10, 20 and 50 cents and 1 and 2 euros.

10 euros

50 euros

200 euros

500 euros

ARRIVING

There are direct international flights into Schiphol Airport from around the world, as well as good rail connections with most European cities and regular sailings from the UK to major ferry ports, all of which have good rail connections to Amsterdam.

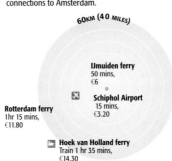

60KM (40 MILES)

IJmuiden ferry
50 mins,
€6

Schiphol Airport
15 mins,
€3.20

Rotterdam ferry
1hr 15 mins,
€11.80

Hoek van Holland ferry
Train 1 hr 35 mins,
€14.30

FROM SCHIPHOL

Schiphol (☎ 0900/0141), Amsterdam's only international airport, is 13km (8 miles) south-west of the heart of the city. Many international airlines operate scheduled and charter flights here. Trains leave the airport for Amsterdam Centraal Station every 15 minutes from 6am until midnight, then hourly through the night. The ride takes 20 minutes and costs €3.20. Connexxion buses run from the airport to a number of big hotels and you do not need to have travelled on the airline or be staying at one of the hotels to use this service. The cost is €8.50 one way. There are between 1 and 3 departures each hour, 7am–9pm (☎ 0900/9292). Taxis are available but fares run as high as €45. It is usually faster to go by train to Centraal Station and take a taxi from there.

ARRIVING BY RAIL

Centraal Station has direct connections from major cities in western Europe, including high-speed links from Paris, Brussels and Cologne. From Britain, there are connections at Brussels with trains operated by Eurostar, with bargain through fares to Amsterdam. Train information: (☎ 0900/9292; www.ns.nl).

ARRIVING BY SEA

The major ferry ports—IJmuiden (23km/14 miles), Rotterdam Europoort (70km/43 miles) and Hoek van Holland (Hook of Holland, 68km/42 miles from Amsterdam)—have good rail connections with Amsterdam. Regular sailings from the UK are offered by Stena Line, DFDS Seaways and P&O Ferries.

GETTING AROUND

Amsterdam has excellent public transport. Distances are short so you can walk or cycle to most places. But on a cold, wet day, you may be grateful to ride, and a tram trip is an attraction in its own right. The same ticket is valid for tram, bus and Metro. If you intend to use public transport frequently, buy a strip card of 15 or 45 units (*strippenkaart*) at Amsterdam's municipal transport authority, GVB and Dutch Railways ticket counters at most stations, and also at the Vereniging voor Vreemdelingenverkeer (VVV) tourist offices (▶ 90–91).

Sixteen different tram lines have frequent services from 6am on weekdays (slightly later on weekends) until midnight, when night buses take over, running hourly until 4am. Day tickets are valid during the night following the day on which they were issued. If you don't have a ticket, on most trams you board towards the rear and pay the conductor. Take care when getting off; many stops are in the middle of the road (▶ 91).

There are four Metro lines, three terminating at Centraal Station, used mainly by commuters from the suburbs. The most useful city-centre stations are Nieuwmarkt and Waterlooplein.

It is difficult to hail a taxi in the street. Go to a taxi stand at major squares, and outside major hotels, tourist attractions and Centraal Station. Taxis are free to charge what they like, so it is essential to ask the driver for an estimate for the journey before you start. Fares are high.

DON'T DRIVE

Driving is not an ideal way of getting about the city because of the scarcity and high cost of public parking, the one-way streets and the large number of cyclists.

VISITORS WITH DISABILITIES

The Netherlands is one of the most progressive countries in the world when it comes to providing access and information. Hotels, museums and buildings that meet minimum standards display the International Accessibility Symbol. Tourist Information Offices have full information on hotels, restaurants, museums, tourist attractions and boat and coach excursions with facilities for people with disabilities. A special taxi service is available for people with disabilities Monday to Friday 9am–5pm (☎ 6333943); reserve at least two days ahead.

For further information contact the Federatie Nederlandse Gehandicaptenraad, Postbus 169, 3500 AD, Utrecht (☎ 030 2313454).

Living
Amsterdam

Amsterdam Now

Above: *Eating and drinking out is popular in Amsterdam*
Right: *Tulips from Amsterdam—bulbs and blooms are sold throughout the city.*

A BOLD IDEA

• Radical politicians of the 1970s came up with the bold idea of providing free bicycles, painted white that everyone could use. The idea floundered when the bikes were stolen, repainted and sold. Now the white bikes are back—but this time they can only be unlocked using an electronic smart card.

To some, Amsterdam conjures the vanilla scent of waffles, barrel organs, carillons ringing out their hymns from church steeples. To others it is synonymous with tolerance—of eccentricity and of experimentation. Some party all night and sleep off their excesses during the day; others studiously walk the canal circle, marvelling at myriad variations on the Dutch gable, or they use Amsterdam as a base for visiting the bulb fields of Haarlem, Edam and Gouda of cheese fame or porcelain-producing Delft.

The city is so small you can cross it in 30 minutes on foot; it is the capital of a country so small that it would fit into Ireland two-and-a-half times over. Amsterdam is tiny—just three quarters of a million people packed into not quite enough space. Yet for all its compact scale, it rewards frequent visits, and it has a changing programme of special exhibitions, festivals and arts events—from the wackiest avant-garde shows to the

Above: *Amsterdam's former stock exchange, the Beurs van Berlage (1903), is now a concert venue and exhibition space*
Left: *Browsing in the shop at the Van Gogh Museum*

works of Rembrandt or Vermeer. The many faces of Amsterdam help make it among Europe's most popular short-break destinations.

For sheer creative energy, few cities can compete. Although the city is surrounded by light industrial estates, many who live in central Amsterdam live off their wits as academics, authors, photographers, artists, architects, journalists, lawyers and musicians. Amsterdam's university adds to the lively and youthful mix. Its various faculties (whose walls are even more plastered with graffiti than most Amsterdam buildings) dominate the city. Many of the city's famous *hofjes*—courtyards, originally built as

THE BELLS

● Amsterdam's carillons, high in church steeples, mark the passing of the hours all over the city by playing everything from hymns to melodies by Mozart or Beethoven. Among the best are the bells of Oude Kerk and of Westerkerk, which gave comfort to Anne Frank while she was in hiding during the 1940s.

Above: Musicians out in force on Queen's Day
Above right: The Bulldog coffee shop

almshouses or for religious communities—are now student housing.

Amsterdam feels like a big village. Many people who live in the heart know each other, if only by sight, and the mayor is even seen on public transport, where he listens in on people's conversations, to find out what they care about; if you stay a few days you are treated as an honorary citizen. Amsterdammers' sociability makes it easy to get to know people—as does the fact that many speak several languages.

QUEEN'S DAY

• Nothing better sums up Amsterdam than Koninginnedag (Queen's Day), the unstuffy monarch's official birthday (30 April) and the occasion for a wild city-wide street party. Even radical Amsterdammers celebrate. Everyone wears orange, the royal colour, and the gay community dons tiaras, tinsel and fancy dress. Over a million people take part.

CYCLE CITY

• First-time visitors to Amsterdam may well be mown down by a speeding bicycle within a few moments of arrival. Designated cycle paths through the city often run contrary to the traffic flow, so you have to look both ways before crossing any road. Soon you can be joining in the fun; using a Dutch 'sit-up-and-beg' bicycle without brakes—instead you have to back pedal —takes skill but soon becomes second nature. Never leave your bicycle unlocked as there is a large amount of bike theft.

Intellectual, curious about the world and great talkers, it is not surprising that Amsterdammers have dared to embark on some of the great social experiments of our time. It sometimes seems that where Amsterdam, with the rest of the Netherlands, leads, the world generally follows—though maybe a few centuries later. Prostitution has been tolerated in Amsterdam since the 17th century, when local officials used to make a small fortune from the sex industry. Amsterdam's liberal drug laws allow licensed cafés to permit the sale of cannabis. Amsterdam

Above: NEMO—the interactive museum of science and technology is also a striking piece of architecture

RECLAIMING THE STREETS

• Little by little, Amsterdam is getting tough on cars and reclaiming run down areas. To celebrate the millennium, the Dam was turned into an Italian-style piazza, from which cars are now banned, though taxis and trams still encircle the perimeter. Next in line to be transformed is Warmoesstraat, once a seedy back street fringing the Red-Light District, now a pedestrianized street with an increasing number of upmarket shops and eateries. It leads to Zeedijk, another street that the city is proud to have regenerated. Amsterdam's Chinese community have now made it their own, complete with the Fo Guang Shan He Hua Buddist Temple. On the nearby waterfront, Renzo Piano's striking ship-like NEMO museum has reclaimed another neglected city corner. The sweeping flight of terraced steps takes you to the pinnacle for unrivalled views.

Above: The Tropenmuseum displays artefacts from the tropical regions of the world, giving a glimpse into the daily life of the inhabitants

invented traffic calming—tough laws and schemes to discourage cars and improve driving conditions—and it may yet become the first city to ban cars outright. Laws permit euthanasia and gay marriages. The Dutch police and military are more liberal than in many a European state, and the Dutch are passionately in favour of greater European integration. The squatter movement colonizes empty buildings and draws attention to the lack of affordable housing within the city. This social liberalism is reflected in Amsterdammers' lifestyle. Informality is the norm—local business people long ago abandoned suits and ties, and most restaurants are refreshingly unpretentious. Many a street corner has a *bruine kroeg* (brown café), named after the mellow hue of the tobacco-stained walls where people comfortably settle down with a newspaper, or play a game of chess, or argue over the issues of the day with friends and regulars. At weekends Amsterdammers make the

TREE STORY

• Satuesque elms once lined Amsterdam's canals, but many succumbed to Dutch elm disease in the 1970s—the beetle-born fungus first identified here. Plane trees, their replacements, withstand city pollution by shedding their bark.

Above: *Amsterdam's oldest church, Oude Kerk, is a haven of spirituality in the midst of the Red-Light District*

most of the recreational opportunities around them: flat land—perfect for cycling—and an abundance of water for swimming, sailing and watersports. People work hard when they need to, but whenever the sun shines, and in this northern latitude and maritime climate the skies more often than not hint at rain, Amsterdammers are out in the streets and enjoying their city—as will you.

LIFE ON THE WATER

• Amsterdam is expanding, to handle a projected increase in population to 800,000 by 2020. Most of the expansion is taking place among what used to be the quays and installations of the city's old harbour, along the IJ waterfront west, east and north of Centraal Station. Cutting-edge modern architecture, often on an untypical-for-Holland gargantuan scale, is the theme of most redeveloped zones, but some space has been kept for refurbished warehouses and other buildings. You can reach these zones where the city's future is taking shape by ferry boats from behind Centraal Station, and on the fast IJ-tram from Centraal Station which entered service in 2005.

DIVERSITY

• Colonial ties with the Dutch East Indies (now Indonesia) and Dutch Guyana (now Surinam) have given Amsterdam a large ethnic population, swelled by immigrants from Turkey and Morocco. Many come to shop at the colourful Albert Cuypstraat street market, jammed with foods and textiles from around the world.

Amsterdam Then

BEFORE 1400

Herring fisherman settle on the Amstel in the 13th century and a dam is built across the river. In 1300 the settlement is given city status and in 1345 becomes a pilgrimage centre and a major trading post although remaining very small.

HERRING CITY

If there had been no herring, Amsterdam might never have come into existence. In the Middle Ages, the Dutch discovered how to cure these fish, and they became a staple food. Herring fishermen built a dam across the Amstel river and a small fishing village developed, Amstelledamme. Its site is now the Dam, Amsterdam's main square.

1425 First horseshoe canal, the Singel, is dug.

1517 Protestant Reformation in Germany. In subsequent decades Lutheran and Calvinist ideas take root in the city.

1519 Amsterdam becomes part of the Spanish empire and nominally Catholic.

1567–68 Start of the Eighty Years' War against Spanish rule.

1578 Amsterdam capitulates to William of Orange. Calvinists take power.

17th century Dutch Golden Age. Amsterdam becomes the most important port in the world.

1602 United East India Company founded.

1613 Work starts on the Gratchtengordel (Canal Ring).

1642 Rembrandt paints his classic work *The Night Watch*.

1648 End of war with Spain.

1652–54 First of a series of wars with Britain for maritime supremacy.

1806 Napoleon takes over the republic.

From left to right: Map of
Amsterdam, c1544;
William I of Orange
(1533–84);
the returning fleet of the
Dutch East India Company in
the 17th century;
Amsterdam Olympics, 1928;
Anne Frank (1929–45)

1813 Prince William returns from exile. Crowned William I in 1814.

1876 North Sea Canal opens, bringing new prosperity.

1928 Amsterdam hosts the Olympics.

1914–18 World War I. Netherlands neutral.

1940–45 German Occupation in World War II. Anne Frank goes into hiding.

1960s–70s Hippies flock to the city from Europe.

1964–67 Anti-establishment riots in the city.

1980 Queen Beatrix crowned. The city is named Holland's capital.

1989 City government falls because of weak anti-vehicle laws. New laws eventually free the city of traffic.

1990 Van Gogh centenary exhibition attracts 890,000 visitors.

1998–99 Redevelopment of Museumplein.

2004 Film maker Theo van Gogh is murdered in Amsterdam after making a film critical of Islam, prompting a national debate about whether tolerance has been taken too far.

A POPULAR MONARCH

Beatrix, Queen of the Netherlands, came to the throne when her mother Queen Juliana, abdicated on 30 April 1980. Beatrix, born in 1938, was crowned at the Nieuwe Kerk. Her great popularity is reflected on her official birthday (*Koninginnedag*, 30 April)—an exuberantly celebrated national holiday.

17

Time to Shop

From flowers to fashions, clocks to souvenirs, there's plenty to see in the shop windows of Amsterdam

Amsterdam is full of fascinating quirky shops specializing in everything from toothbrushes to aboriginal art, children's comics to art-deco lamps, potted plants to exotic cut flowers, jazz CDs to cheese, beer or African masks. These shops are not always in the obvious places.

CLUMPING CLOGS

Think Amsterdam and you'll probably think of clogs—or *klompen* as they are known in Dutch, a splendidly onomatopoeic word that imitates the heavy clumping sound the wooden shoes make as they stroll the city's pavements. They are carved from a single block of poplar wood and are extremely comfortable. Most however are sold as decorative souvenirs rather than as footwear. You'll find these painted with windmills, tulips or cheeses.

Amsterdam's main shopping streets—Nieuwendijk and Kalverstraat—are dominated by global brands. Instead look where rents are lower: along Haarlemmerstraat, Damstraat and in the cross streets of the Canal Circle and the Jordaan. These cross streets were deliberately zoned for commercial use in the 17th century, when the canal circle was planned and thrived on the trade in furs and hides. Just go and wander down Reestraat, Hartenstraat, Berenstraat, Runstraat and Huidenstraat among the medley of small specialist shops, cafés and art galleries, which have replaced the original furriers.

The entrepreneurs who run these shops have a passion for their product and they want to share their enthusiasm, so customers are not treated merely as consumers, but as fellow connoisseurs. Some will happily spend all day talking about their sources. Others are busy making the products they sell—gorgeously decorated hats, Venetian-style masks, recycled vintage clothing, evening dresses or costume jewellery.

The range of specialities and what they say about human ingenuity is incredible. If it's chocolate you want, go and talk to Hendrikse, the owner of Le Confiseur (✉ Overtoom 448–50) who produces a wonderful range of handmade truffles as well as sculpted chocolate

figures of people and animals. Feeling guilty about consuming all that sugar? De Witte Tandenwinkel (✉ Runstraat 5) sells every imaginable colour of toothbrush and every possible flavour of toothpaste. Olivaria (✉ Hazenstraat 2A) is devoted to olive oils and De Jongejans (✉ Noorderkerkstraat 18) to eyewear—everything from vintage frames and mirrored shades to glam-rock extravaganzas. Joe's Vliegerwinkel (✉ Nieuwe Hoogstraat 19) sells only toys that fly—colourful kites, boomerangs and frisbees. Lovers of children's and adults' comics, new and second-hand, should visit Lambiek (✉ Kerkstraat 119).

You will find more flowers and bulbs in Amsterdam than any other European city—not just in the Floating Flower Market, but all around the Canal Circle. What better souvenir of your stay than a bouquet of blooms—always buy blooms that are still closed—or a packet of bulbs, but be sure to check the import regulations first.

FLEA MARKETS

The dark days of World War II engendered a habit of thrift in the citizens of Amsterdam, and even in today's prosperous times, no true Amsterdammer ever throws anything away. Instead, everything—from dead light bulbs to ancient newspapers—gets recycled at one of the city's many flea markets. The biggest and best known is the one that surrounds two sides of the Stadhuis (Town Hall) on Waterlooplein. Stalls here mix the new, the old and the unimaginably decrepit. Pick up very serviceable second-hand clothes, craft items and jewellery, and wonder why anyone would want to buy a broken radio, chipped vase or a doll without a head. Other flea markets: De Looier, Rommelmarkt and the market at Noordermarkt.

Out and About

SIGHTSEEING TOURS

WATER TOURS
Holland International
✉ Prins Hendrikkade 33a
☎ 6227788. Cruises
every 15 mins in summer;
every 30 mins in winter.
Canal Bus
✉ Weteringschans 24
☎ 6239886. Water-bus
service around the city.
Lovers
✉ Prins Hendrikkade
opposite 25, near Centraal
Station
☎ 6222181. Tours daily
10–5, every 30 mins.
Museumboot
✉ Stationsplein 8
☎ 6222181. Links six
jetties near the 20 major
museums. Service every
30–45 mins.

BICYCLE TOURS
Yellow Bike Tours
✉ Nieuwezijds Kolk 29
☎ 6206940

WALKING TOURS
Mee in Mokum
✉ Hartenstraat 18
☎ 6251390. Tours
Tue–Sun 11am (2-3
hours).

ITINERARIES
HISTORIC CITY
Start by visiting the Amsterdams Historisch Museum (➤ 37) to get an idea of the city's colourful history. Then stop at the Begijnhof (➤ 36), Holland's finest almshouses. For lunch try Caffé Esprit (➤ 71), a smart designer café popular with shoppers, or a Dutch restaurant, such as Haesje Claes (➤ 64). After lunch enjoy the street entertainment between visits to the sumptuous Koninklijk Paleis (Royal Palace ➤ 38) and Nieuwe Kerk (➤ 39), both on the Dam (now a square) that gave Amsterdam its name. Having booked in advance, if possible, go to a classical music concert at the Concertgebouw (➤ 56 and 80) or Beurs van Berlage, or take in a performance of opera or dance at the Muziektheater (➤ 57, 79 and 80).

MARITIME HISTORY
It's easy to imagine 17th-century Amsterdam at the peak of its maritime success during an early morning stroll around the Western Islands (➤ 53). A bus ride from here (nos. 22, 32) takes you to the Eastern Islands and the Scheepvaart Museum (➤ 49). For lunch try the museum restaurant. Then head for the Tropenmuseum (➤ 50), which re-creates tropical scenes, or walk to the Hortus Botanicus (➤ 60), the botanical gardens with more than 8,000 plant species, close to Artis Zoo (➤ 61). Continue to the Museum Willet-Holthuysen (➤ 45), built for a wealthy Golden Age merchant. In the evening take a candlelit cruise and see the Golden Age buildings and canal bridges lit up.

EXCURSIONS
KEUKENHOF GARDENS

These gardens—whose name means 'kitchen gardens'—at the heart of the *Bloembollenstreek* (bulb-growing region) rank among the most famous in the world. The site was used for market gardening until a consortium of bulb-growers realized the tourist potential of a site close to Amsterdam, and the 28ha (69 acres) of woodland park at Lisse were acquired in 1949 as a showcase. Visit between March and late May, when more than seven million bulbs are in bloom, laid out in brilliant swathes of red, yellow, pink and blue. Few people leave without a bag of bulbs for their own garden.

DELFT

This charming old town is known the world over for its blue-and-white pottery. In 1652 there were 32 thriving potteries; today there are just three. Delft was also the birthplace of the artist Johannes Vermeer (1632–75). His simple grave can be seen in the Oude Kerk along with those of other eminent Delft citizens, including Antoine van Leeuwenhoek, inventor of the microscope (1632–1723).

William of Orange lead his revolt against Spanish rule from the Prinsenhof in Delft. The building now houses the city museum, which includes a collection of rare antique Delftware. Up the stairs you can still see the holes made by the bullets that killed William in 1584. His marble tomb, designed by Hendrick de Keyser in 1614, lies in the Nieuwe Kerk.

From left to right:
Historic barges outside NEMO museum;
the view from the city's canals;
the best time to visit Keukenhof is in the spring;
a variety of plates, vases and other articles in the unmistakable blue-glazed Delftware

INFORMATION

KEUKENHOF
Distance 26km (16 miles) southwest
Travel time 1 hour
🚍 Combined rail/bus/admission tickets from Centraal Station
✉ Lisse
☎ 0252/465596

DELFT
Distance 55km (34 miles) southwest
Travel time 1 hour
🚆 Train from Centraal Station to The Hague then change for Delft
ℹ Hippolytusbuurt 4
☎ 015/2154051;
www.delft.nl

21

Walks

INFORMATION

Distance 4km (2.5 miles)
Time 1–2 hours
Start/End point ★ Dam
🚊 Tram 4, 9, 14, 16, 24, 25

THE CANAL RING AND JORDAAN

Leave the Dam via Paleisstraat; continue straight on over the scenic Singel, Herengracht and Keizersgracht canals, and then turn right alongside Prinsengracht to pass the high tower of the Westerkerk and the Anne Frankhuis (Anne Frank's House). Cross over Prinsengracht and double back for a few metres along the west bank of the canal until you reach the peaceful Bloemgracht canal. Turn right here, take the second right up Tweede Leliedwarsstraat, cross over Egelantiersgracht, and turn right along its shady bank and then left up Tweede Egelantiersdwarsstraat into the heart of the bohemian Jordaan district.

Walk on to Lijnbaansgracht, and then turn right into Lindengracht, once a canal and now site of a Saturday food market, to Brouwersgracht (► 52), lined with traditional barges and houseboats. Cross Brouwersgracht at Herengracht and continue along Brouwersgracht to the Singel. Cross by the sluice gates and turn right along the eastern side of the Singel, past Amsterdam's narrowest house façade (No. 7). To conclude the walk, turn left at Torenstraat, cross Spui and go along Molensteeg. Continue across Nieuwezijds Voorburgwal, past Nieuwe Kerk on the left and return to the Dam.

0   500 m

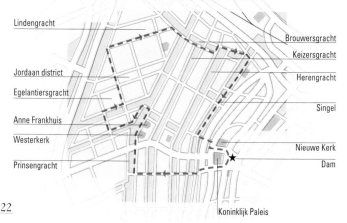

Lindengracht

Brouwersgracht

Keizersgracht

Jordaan district

Herengracht

Egelantiersgracht

Anne Frankhuis

Singel

Westerkerk

Nieuwe Kerk

Prinsengracht

Dam

Koninklijk Paleis

MARKETS AND MUSEUMS

Leaving the Dam via Paleisstraat, turn left into Nieuwezijds Voorburgwal, where a stamp and coin market is held (► 55). About 100m (100 yards) farther on the left, Sint-Luciënsteeg leads to the Amsterdams Historisch Museum. Pass through the Schuttersgalerij (Civic Guard Gallery) to a lane of whitewashed houses called Gedempte Begijnensloot. At the southern end, a stone archway on your right brings you into the leafy, cobbled, Begijnhof courtyard. A further archway leads to Spui and its pavement cafés. On Fridays, stalls sell antiquarian books, and on Sundays paintings and prints.

Head southwest from Spui and turn left along the edge of the Singel. Cross the bridge into Koningsplein and Amsterdam's flower market, the Bloemenmarkt. Your next landmark is the Munttoren at Muntplein. Turn right and follow the Amstel just past the Blauwbrug (Blue Bridge). Turn right along Herengracht for a short detour to the Willet-Holthuysen Museum, an elegant patrician mansion. On your return, cross the bridge to reach the Waterlooplein flea market. Tucked away at the far end of the market is the Museum Het Rembrandthuis, which is not to be missed. After your walk have a drink on the terrace of Café Dantzig (► 70).

INFORMATION

Distance 2.5km (1.5 miles)
Time 1–2 hours
Start point ★ Dam
🚋 Tram 4, 9, 14, 16, 24, 25
End point Museum het Rembrandthuis
🚇 Waterlooplein

0   1 km

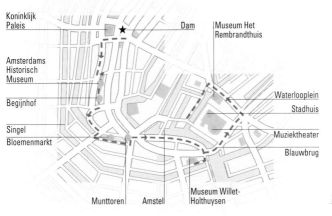

Koninklijk Paleis
Dam
Museum Het Rembrandthuis
Amsterdams Historisch Museum
Waterlooplein
Stadhuis
Begijnhof
Singel
Bloemenmarkt
Muziektheater
Blauwbrug
Munttoren   Amstel
Museum Willet-Holthuysen

23

Amsterdam by Night

Above: *The Concertgebouw,
built in 1888, looks beautiful
illuminated at night.*
Above right: *Café-club in
Rembrandtplein*

CITY OF JAZZ

Amsterdam's theme tune
is the wail of a jazz saxo-
phone mingling with the
keening of seagulls. This is
a city that adores jazz and
blues, and there are scores
of venues to chose from,
including the legendary
Bimhuis (which moved in
2005 to the new
Muziekgebouw aan 't IJ)
and Maloe Melo. The city
hosts the International
Blues Festival in mid-
March (www.meervaart.
nl), although it cedes to
The Hague (Den Haag) the
honour of hosting the
renowned North Sea Jazz
Festival in mid-July (www.
northseajazz.nl). Both
attract huge international
stars—and aficionados
flock from all over Europe
to hear them.

Amsterdam is one of Europe's most vibrant
nightlife capitals. On a mild summer's evening
nothing beats just walking by the canal, or glid-
ing along the canals in a glass-topped boat, to
see the historic bridges and buildings spot-
lighted or outlined in white lights. Alternatively
sit out of doors to enjoy a drink at a canalside
café or stop at a brown café or two (➤ 82). For
those who prefer a romantic dinner the choice is
tremendous, with Indonesian cuisine a favourite.

There is plenty going on at the cinemas, both
mainstream and art house. Don't miss the
Tuschinski Theater (➤ 79). It is a splendid elaborate art-deco style building, and for the priciest
tickets you get a glass of champagne included.

Book in advance to hear some of the world's
leading orchestras (➤ 80). Even if you don't plan
ahead, there is always something going on—many
churches host choral concerts and organ recitals, the
Melkweg and Paradiso nightclubs have rock and
pop, Maloe Melo (➤ 81) has blues and rock, the
new Muziekgebouw aan't IJ has the former
Muziekcentrum De IKbreker experimental music
venue and, in an adjacent hall, the Bimhius has jazz.

The city's nightclubs offer all kinds of entertainment,
including plenty that is explicitly erotic in the Red-
Light District. Leidseplein and Rembrandtplein
throng with pre-party drinkers; they head for Escape
(✉ Rembrandtplein 11), one of Europe's biggest
and best-known clubs, or Club iT (✉ Amstelstraat
24), where beautiful people either wear very few
clothes or dress up like actors in a Fellini film.

AMSTERDAM's
top 25 sights

Vondelpark

Open-air auditorium in Vondelpark

This is a popular place for sunbathers, joggers, frisbee-throwers and book-worms—great for people-watching. Be entertained by musicians, mime artists and acrobats in this welcome splash of green near the heart of the city.

Pleasure gardens With its wide open spaces, fragrant rose garden, playgrounds, bandstand and cafés, Vondelpark is a popular place of escape from the busy city streets. Amsterdam's largest and oldest municipal park—a 48-ha (118-acre) rectangle of former marshland—was first opened in 1865. The designers, J. D. and L. P. Zocher, intentionally moved away from the symmetrical Dutch garden, creating in the romantic English style with lengthy pathways, open lawns, ornamental lakes, meadows and woodland containing 120 varieties of tree, including catalpa, chestnut, cypress, oak and poplar. Financed by wealthy local residents, the Nieuwe Park (as it was then called) became the heart of a luxurious new residential district, overlooked by elegant town houses and villas. Two years later, a statue of Holland's best-known playwright, Joost van den Vondel (1587–1679) was erected in the park and its present name was adopted. It is the only city park in Holland that has been designated a listed monument. It also has the historical archives and working cinema of the Nederlands Filmmuseum.

Like a summer-long pop festival The heyday of the Vondelpark was in the 1970s, when hippies flocked to Amsterdam, attracted by the city's tolerance for soft drugs. Vondelpark soon became their main gathering place. The bubble burst at the end of the decade and the hippies dispersed. All that now remains are street musicians, flea markets and the occasional ageing hippy.

Van Gogh Museum

It is a moving experience to trace Vincent Van Gogh's tragic life and extraordinary achievement, through such a varied display of his art, his Japanese prints and his contemporary works.

World's largest Van Gogh collection Of his 900 paintings and 1,200 drawings, the Van Gogh Museum has 200 and 500 respectively, together with 850 letters, Vincent's fine Japanese prints and works by friends and influential contemporaries, including Gauguin, Monet, Bernard and Pissarro. Van Gogh's paintings are arranged chronologically, starting with works from 1880 to 1887, a period characterized by realistic landscape paintings and peasant scenes in heavy tones. This period is typified by *The Potato Eaters* (1885).

Colourful palette The broad brush strokes and bold colours that characterize van Gogh's works of 1887–90 show the influence of his 1886 move to Paris and the effect of Impressionism, most striking in street and café scenes. Tired of city life, he moved in 1888 to Arles where, intoxicated by the intense sunlight and the brilliant colours of Provence, he painted many of his finest works, including *Harvest at La Crau* and the *Sunflowers* series. After snipping off a bit of his ear and offering it to a local prostitute, Van Gogh voluntarily entered an asylum in St.-Rémy, where his art took an expressionistic form. His mental anguish may be seen in the way he painted gnarled trees and menacing skies, as in the desolate *Wheatfield with Crows*. At the age of 37, he shot himself.

Extra space Temporary and special exhibitions are mounted in an ellipse-shaped wing by Japanese architect Kisho Kurokawa and opened in 1999 on Museumplein, behind the main museum.

HIGHLIGHTS

- *The Potato Eaters* (1885)
- *Bedroom at Arles* (1888)
- *Vase with Sunflowers* (1888)
- *Wheatfield with Crows* (1890)

DID YOU KNOW?

- Van Gogh sold only one painting in his lifetime
- Record price for a Van Gogh painting is €37.125 million (1990 *Portrait of Dr. Gachet*)

INFORMATION

www.vangoghmuseum.nl
- ✉ Paulus Potterstraat 7
- ☎ 5705200
- ◉ Daily 10–6. Closed 1 Jan
- 🍴 Self-service restaurant
- 🚊 Tram 2, 3, 5, 12, 16
- 🚢 Museumboat stop 6
- ♿ Excellent 💲 Expensive
- ↔ Rijksmuseum (▶ 28)

Top: Bedroom at Arles
Below: Self-portrait

Rijksmuseum 'De Meesterwerken'

HIGHLIGHTS

- *The Night Watch*, Rembrandt (1642)
- *The Jewish Bride*, Rembrandt (1665)
- *The Milk Maid*, Vermeer (1658)
- *The Love Letter*, Vermeer (1670)
- 17th-century doll houses

INFORMATION

www.rijksmuseum.nl

- ✉ Jan Luijkenstraat 1
- ☎ 6477000
- 🕐 Daily 9–6. Closed 1 Jan
- 🚊 Tram 2, 5
- 🚢 Museumboat stop 6
- ♿ Very good
- 💷 Expensive
- ↔ Van Gogh Museum (➤ 27); Leidseplein (➤ 29)

Even in this shruken state, the Rijksmuseum's Masterpieces collection is a glorious evocation of the Dutch Golden Age.

Old Masters Holand's most important museum is operating on a limited basis until 2008, while most of the building is being refurbished. But even when it was fully open, the Rijksmuseum could display only a fraction of its collection. Now that it has been reduced to just the Philips Wing, to the rear of the main building, the lack of exhibition space is worse than acute. The solution has been to display only the finest paintings of the 17th-century Old Masters and other pieces from this period. Pride of place goes to Rembrandt's *The Night Watch* (1642). This vast, dramatic canvas—one of his largest and most famous compositions, portraying an Amsterdam militia company—is a showpiece of 17th-century Dutch art. In other rooms hang more works by Rembrandt and by his pupils. Jan Steen, Johannes Vermeer and Frans Hals also feature prominently. Along with the remarkable Dutch paintings, the treasures on display include a collection of Delftware and two ingeniously made doll's houses—scaled down copies of old canal houses, with sumptuous 17th-century period furnishings

Design masterpiece Although most of the Rijksmuseum building is closed, it's still worthwhile to peruse the architecture, even from a distance. The palatial red-brick building was designed by Petrus Josephus Hubertus Cuypers and opened in 1885. It is mostly in the style known as Dutch neo-Renaissance, but Cuypers slipped in some neo-Gothic touches that give the building a cathedral-esque air—which was greatly to the annoyance of King William III.

Leidseplein

This square represents Amsterdam's nightlife at its most vibrant. It is filled with street cafés, ablaze with neon and abuzz with street entertainers.

Party district for centuries During the Middle Ages, farmers on their way to market unloaded their carts here, at the outskirts of the city. At the turn of the 19th century, artists and writers gathered here. In the 1930s Leidseplein was the site of many clashes between political factions, and it became the main site of anti-Nazi rallies during the war. In the 1960s it was the stomping ground of the *Pleiners* (Dutch Mods), and in 1992 it witnessed wild celebrations following local football team Ajax's UEFA Cup victory. Today, despite the constant flow of trams through the square, you are almost sure to find fire-eaters, sword-swallowers and other street entertainers, both good and bad. By night, dazzling neon lights and crowded café terraces seating over 1,000 people transform the square into an Amsterdam hot spot, busy until the early hours. Be sure to spend at least one evening here. Look for two notable buildings, both protected monuments: the distinctive, attractive red-brick Stadsschouwburg (Municipal Theatre), with its wide verandah and little turrets, and the art nouveau American Hotel, with its striking art deco Café Américain.

Winter wonderland Whatever the season, Leidseplein remains one of the city's main meeting places. In winter, when most tourists have departed, it becomes quintessentially Dutch. Most of the outdoor café terraces disappear and locals huddle together for a drink and a chat in heated covered terraces, or inside the cafés. It is also *the* place to be to take part in New Year's Eve celebrations.

HIGHLIGHTS

- American Hotel (1904)
- Stadsschouwburg (1894)
- Street entertainment

INFORMATION

- ✉ Leidseplein
- 🍴 Restaurants and cafés
- 🚊 Tram 1, 2, 5, 6, 7, 10, 20
- 🚢 Museumboat stop 5
- ↔ Vondelpark (► 26), Prinsengracht (► 31)

Top: Cafés in Leidseplein by night. Below: A stilt walker entertains

Woonbootmuseum

HIGHLIGHTS

- Browsing the houseboat library
- Watching the slide show
- Sipping coffee in the café corner at the same eye level as the ducks

INFORMATION

www. houseboatmuseum.nl

✉ Prinsengracht opposite No. 296, facing Elandsgracht

☎ 4270750

🕐 Mar–end Oct Wed–Sun 11–5; Nov–end Feb Fri–Sun 11–5. Closed 1 Jan, 30 Apr, 25, 26, 31 Dec

🍴 Café

🚊 Tram 6, 13, 14, 17

♿ None

💶 Inexpensive

Some 2,500 houseboats line the canals of Amsterdam, homes to people who prefer the alternative lifestyle of being afloat. The Houseboat Museum is an invitation to find out just what appeals about a floating home.

Home from home The Houseboat Museum feels exactly like someone's home, and the question that visitors most often ask is whether somebody still lives aboard the *Hendrika Maria*, a retired canal barge built in 1914. In fact, nobody does, but visitors are invited to pretend that they do: In this museum you are allowed to make yourself at home, sit in the comfortable armchairs and browse the books that line the walls of the surprisingly spacious living area.

High maintenance Another common reaction is: 'I'd love to live on a boat like this'. The museum provides plenty of information about houseboat living to encourage such dreams but warns about the rising price of moorings in Amsterdam. The slide show makes it clear that maintaining a houseboat is a labour of love. Every three to four years the boat has to be taken out of the water and pressure hosed to remove corrosive accretions. Loose rivets have to be replaced and even whole sections of hull if they become thin.

Rising costs When all the costs are added up, houseboat living is not substantially cheaper than living in an equivalent sized apartment. What began as an inexpensive alternative lifestyle in the 1960s is now a costly commitment. But people who live on boats are passionate and would not have it any other way. The museum provides an insight into life aboard through an entertaining slide show, the numerous publications for sale and the boat itself.

Prinsengracht

Of the three canals that form the Grachtengordel (Canal Ring), Prinsengracht is in many ways the most atmospheric, with its fine merchants' homes, converted warehouses and flower-laden houseboats.

Prince William's canal Prinsengracht (Prince's Canal), named after William of Orange, was dug at the same time as Herengracht and Keizersgracht as part of a massive 17th-century expansion scheme. Together these three form the city's distinctive horseshoe-shaped canal network. Less exclusive than the other two waterways, with smaller houses, Prinsengracht became an important thoroughfare lined with warehouses and merchants' homes. Cargo would be unloaded from ships into fourth-floor storehouses by means of the massive hoist-beams seen today in the gables of many buildings (and still used for lifting furniture). Some houses were built with a deliberate tilt, to protect their façades from the goods as they were hoisted.

Floating homes Today, you'll also see some of Amsterdam's most beautiful houseboats moored along Prinsengracht, near Brouwersgracht and alongside the ivy-covered quays close to the Amstel. Amsterdammers have long lived on houseboats, but the housing crisis after World War II skyrocketed the population of boat-people, so that there are more than 2,500 legal houseboats in Amsterdam, all with a postal address and power hook-ups. The unofficial figure is a lot higher. You can see a variety of craft on Prinsengracht, some more seaworthy than others, ranging from solid old Rhine barges to chalet-like rafts, boats with greenhouses and gardens and trendy studio homes.

HIGHLIGHTS

- Amstelkerk (➤ 59)
- Anne Frankhuis (➤ 33)
- Noorderkerk (➤ 59)
- Noordermarkt (➤ 55)
- Westerkerk (➤ 32)

DID YOU KNOW?

- Prinsengracht is 4.5km (3 miles) long, 2m (6ft) deep and 25m (80ft) wide to accommodate four lanes of shipping
- A law (dating from 1565) restricts the lean of canal houses to 1:25

INFORMATION

- 🍴 Bars, cafés, restaurants
- 🚊 Tram 1, 2, 4, 5, 6, 13, 14, 16, 17, 24, 25
- 🚢 Museumboat stop 2
- 🔄 Herengracht (➤ 34), Anne Frankhuis (➤ 33), Westerkerk (➤ 32); Woonbootmuseum (➤ 30)

Westerkerk

DID YOU KNOW?

- The church was consecrated in 1631
- The tower contains a carillon of 48 bells
- The largest bell weighs 7,500kg (16,500lb) and its hammer weight is 200kg (440lb)

INFORMATION

www.westerkerk.nl

✉ Prinsengracht 281, Westermarkt

☎ Church 6247766, tower 6126856

🕓 Church Apr–end Sep Mon–Fri 11-3; tower Apr–end Sep Mon–Fri 10–5

🚊 Tram 6, 13, 14, 17

🚤 Museumboat stop 2

♿ Few

🎫 Inexpensive (tower)

↔ Prinsengracht (► 31), Anne Frankhuis (► 33)

❓ Carillon concerts most Tue at noon

This is the most beautiful of the four churches built in the 17th century to the north, south, east and west of the city's core. The views from the tall tower are unsurpassable and make the 85-m (280-ft) climb worthwhile.

Masterwork The West Church, the church most visited by tourists in the city, has the largest nave of any Dutch Protestant church, and the tallest tower and largest congregation in Amsterdam. It is the masterwork of Dutch architect Hendrick de Keyser, who died in 1621, one year after construction began. Designed to serve the wealthy bourgeoisie living in the stylish new mansions of the Canal Ring, it was eventually completed by his son Pieter with Cornelis Dancker in 1631. To its tower they added the gaudy golden crown—a symbol of the city granted by Habsburg Emperor Maximilian 150 years earlier. The sweeping views over the Prinsengracht gables can be seen from the tower, popularly called 'Lange Jan' (Tall John). Outside the church, people often lay wreaths at the foot of the statue of Anne Frank (► 33), who used to listen to the church carillon while she was in hiding, before the bells were melted down by the Nazis.

Interior The simple, whitewashed interior is laid out in the shape of a double Greek cross. The massive organ is decorated with musical instruments and frescos of the Evangelists by Gerard de Lairesse, who was one of Rembrandt's pupils. Rembrandt himself was buried here on 8 October 1669. Although no trace of his pauper's grave remains, there is a memorial to him in the north aisle, near the grave of his son, Titus. The church's opening hours for visitors are not guaranteed; it may be closed at the times stated.

Anne Frankhuis

'My greatest wish is to be a journalist, and later on, a famous writer... I'd like to publish a book called 'The Secret Annexe'. It remains to be seen whether I'll succeed, but my diary can serve as a basis.'

Unfulfilled wish On Thursday 11 May 1944, just under three months before she was captured by the Nazis, Anne Frank wrote these poignant words in her diary. She never saw it published, but died in the concentration camp at Bergen-Belsen near the end of World War II, aged 15.

'The Secret Annexe' After Nazi Germany invaded the Netherlands in 1940, increasingly severe anti-Semitic measures were introduced. In 1942, the Frank and van Daan families went into hiding. For the next two years, Anne Frank kept a diary describing daily life and the families' isolation and fear of discovery—until they were betrayed to the Nazis in 1944. Her father was the only member of the group to survive. In 1947, following her wishes, he published her diary, calling it *Het Achterhuis* (The Secret Annexe). Today, over half a million visitors annually make their way through the revolving bookcase that conceals the entrance into the small, gloomy rooms so vividly described in the diary. Mementos on the walls include a map showing the Allied armies' advance from Normandy. Pencilled lines mark the children's growth. The building is preserved by the Anne Frank Foundation, an organization founded to combat racism and anti-Semitism and to promote 'the ideals set down in the Diary of Anne Frank'. In one entry Anne wrote: 'I want to go on living even after my death!' Thanks to her diary, this wish, at least, came true.

HIGHLIGHTS

● The Nazis occupied Amsterdam for five years
● Of Holland's 140,000 pre-war Jewish population only 16,000 survived

INFORMATION

www.annefrank.nl
✉ Prinsengracht 263
☎ 5567105
🕐 Apr–end Aug daily 9–9; Sep–end Mar 9–7 (4 May 9–7, 16 and 31 Dec 9–5, 25 Dec noon–5, 1 Jan noon–7)
🚊 Tram 6, 13, 14, 17
🚢 Museumboat stop 7
♿ None 💷 Expensive
❓ 5-minute introductory film

Top: The revolving bookcase. Below: Sculpture of Anne Frank

Herengracht

Exploring the city's grandest canal is like going back through time to Amsterdam's Golden Age. These gilded houses are a case study of four centuries of Dutch architectural styles.

DID YOU KNOW?

- If you stand on the bridge at the junction of Herengracht and Reguliersgracht, you can see 15 bridges simultaneously

Top: A bell gable beside the Herengracht

The Gentlemen's Canal Herengracht takes its name from the rich merchants and traders of Amsterdam's heyday, and was the first of three concentric canals dug early in the 17th century to house the city's fast-growing population. Attracting the wealthiest merchant aristocrats, it has the largest, most ostentatious houses, 400 of which are now protected monuments. The houses had to conform to many building standards. Even the colour of the front doors—known as Amsterdam green—was regulated. As on all canals, taxes were levied according to the width of the canal frontage, hence the rows of tall, narrow residences.

Gable-spotting Canal house-owners expressed themselves in the elaborate decoration of their houses' gables and façades, and you can find every imaginable design along Herengracht. The earliest and most common are the *step* gable and the *spout* gable. Amsterdam's first *neck* gable (No. 168) was built in 1638 by Philips Vingboons, and the *bell* gable became popular early in the 18th century. Around this time, Louis XIV-style façades were considered the height of fashion. No. 475 is a fine example—nicknamed the jewel of canal houses.

The Golden Bend Amsterdam's most extravagant mansions, with double fronts, were built between Leidsestraat and Vijzelstraat, along the stretch of the canal since dubbed the 'Golden Bend'. To this day, it remains the most prestigious address in town.

Singel

At first glance, this canal looks like any other major waterway in the city. Look a little closer, though, and you will discover some of Amsterdam's most unusual and enchanting sights.

Former city belt From its construction in the early 15th century until the late 16th century, the city limits were marked by the Singel (originally *Cingle*, meaning belt), the city's defensive moat. Then, in 1586, the city council decided to build quays along the Singel's west bank and to convert the moat into a canal for large freight ships. Thus the Singel became the first of Amsterdam's concentric canals, and its curved shape established the horseshoe layout of the city. With the coming of the railways, canal transport became less important and the Singel began to acquire a more residential character. Many warehouses are now converted into homes. The Nieuwe Haarlemmersluis, a sluice at the junction of Singel and Brouwersgracht, is opened nightly to top up the city's canals.

All that floats Perhaps the most unusual house is No. 7. The narrowest house front in Amsterdam, it was made no wider than a door in order to minimise property taxes (➤ 34). Opposite is the *Poezenboot*, a houseboat that is a refuge for stray cats. Lookout, too, for the Torensluis (Tower Lock, on the Singel's widest bridge); in the 17th century it was used as a prison. The bridge has a monument to Multatuli (1820–87), one of the Netherlands' greatest writers. Europe's only floating flower market, the Bloemenmarkt (which doesn't entirely float), is also on the Singel.

HIGHLIGHTS

- Poezenboot
- Bloemenmarkt (➤ 40)
- Torensluis prison cell
- Munttoren (➤ 57)
- No. 7: narrowest house façade
- No. 2, 36, 74, 83: unusual façades

INFORMATION

- ✉ Singel
- ☎ Poezenboot 6258794; www.poezenboot.nl
- 🕐 Poezenboot daily 1–3pm
- 🍴 Cafés and restaurants
- 🚋 Tram 1, 2, 5, 6, 13, 14, 17
- 🚢 Museumboat stop 4
- ♿ Poezenboot none
- 🎫 Poezenboot free
- ↔ Bloemenmarkt (➤ 40), Herengracht (➤ 34), Koninklijk Paleis (➤ 38), Begijnhof (➤ 36)

The Bloemenmarkt brings a riot of colour to the Singel

Begijnhof

Tranquillity characterizes Amsterdam's many *hofjes* (almshouses), none more so than this leafy oasis. The cobbled courtyard, with houses resembling doll's houses, looks like a film set.

DID YOU KNOW?

- The last Begijn died in 1971
- The Pilgrim Fathers are said to have worshipped here before crossing the Atlantic in the *Mayflower*

INFORMATION

- ✉ Gedempte Begijnensloot (entrance in Spui)
- 🕐 Daily 8am–1pm
- 🚊 Tram 1, 2, 5
- 🚢 Museumboat stop 4
- ♿ Good
- 🎫 Free
- ↔ Amsterdams Historisch Museum (➤ 37), Singel (➤ 35)

Below: One of Amsterdam's oldest buildings, The Wooden House

Pious women A tiny, unlikely looking gateway leads to the Begijnhof, the oldest and finest *hofje* in the country (almshouses were charitable lodgings for the poor). This secluded community of magnificently restored old houses and gardens clustered around a small church lies a stone's throw from the main shopping thoroughfare. It was built in 1346 as a sanctuary for the *Begijnen* or Beguines, unmarried women who wanted to live in a religious community without becoming nuns. In return for modest lodging, they devoted themselves to the care of the poor and sick. Today, the Begijnhof is a residence for single women earning less than €16,000 a year, and has a five-year waiting list.

Two churches The Begijnkerk (1419), dominating the courtyard, was confiscated from the Beguines during the Protestant Alteration in 1578. The women continued to worship secretly until religious tolerance was restored over 200 years later, in 1795. Meanwhile, their precious church became a warehouse until 1607, when it was given to the city's Scottish Presbyterian community and renamed (or misnamed) the Engelse Kerk (English Church). The simple interior has pulpit panels by Piet Mondrian. Nearby, Het Houten Huys (The Wooden House, 1425) is one of only two remaining wood-fronted houses in Amsterdam. It was built before 1521, when the use of wood as a building material was banned, after a series of fires. Look for a nearby courtyard, with walls dotted with gable stones saved from demolished Begijnhof houses.

Amsterdams Historisch Museum

Do make this lively and informative museum your first port of call. Once you have a grasp of Amsterdam's colourful history, walks around town are all the more rewarding.

The building This excellent museum traces the growth of Amsterdam from 13th-century fishing village to bustling metropolis, through an impressive collection of paintings, maps, models and historical artefacts. They are displayed chronologically in one of the city's oldest buildings. Originally a monastery, it was occupied by the city orphanage (Burgerweeshuis) for nearly 400 years, until 1975, when it was converted into a museum. Most of the present structure dates from the 16th and 17th centuries. Throughout, you can still see evidence of its former use—notably the ceiling paintings in the Regent's Chamber and the numerous portraits of children, including Jan Carel van Speyck, who later became a Dutch naval hero.

The collections The first rooms of the museum chronicle the city's early history and its rise to prominence in trade and commerce. The displays include furniture, memorabilia and a map that illuminates each 25-year period of growth through the centuries. The museum's main focus is on the Golden Age and colonial expansion. Paintings and photographs illustrate the growing welfare problems of the 19th and early 20th centuries, and a small collection of relics from World War II shows how the Nazi occupation affected the city's population, 10 per cent of which was Jewish. A section focuses on the 'Modern City'. Finally, in the adjoining Schuttersgalerij, don't miss the portraits of the dapper Civic Guard, an armed civilian force formed in the late 14th century to police the city.

HIGHLIGHTS

- *View of Amsterdam,* Cornelis Anthonisz (1538), the oldest city map
- *The Meal of the 17 Guardsmen of Company H,* Cornelis Anthonisz (1533), in the Schuttersgalerij
- *The First Steamship on the IJ,* Nicolaas Bauo (1816)
- *Governesses at the Burgher Orphanage,* Adriaen Backer (1683)
- *Girls from the Civic Orphanage,* Nicolaas van der Waay (1880)
- Bell room

INFORMATION

www.ahm.nl

- ✉ Kalverstraat 92, Nieuwzijds Voorburgwal 357, Sint-Luciënsteeg 27
- ☎ 5231822
- 🕐 Mon–Fri 10–5, Sat–Sun 11–5. Closed 1 Jan, 30 Apr, 25 Dec
- 🍴 David and Goliath Café
- 🚊 Tram 1, 2, 4, 5, 9, 14, 16, 24, 25
- 🚢 Museumboat stop 4
- ♿ Good 💶 Expensive
- 🔄 Koninklijk Paleis (➤ 38)
- ❓ Guided tours on request: telephone in advance

Top: Armour on display in the Amsterdams Historisch Museum

Koninklijk Paleis

Don't be put off by the Royal Palace's sober exterior. It belies the lavish decoration inside—a reminder of the wealth of Amsterdam in its heyday.

HIGHLIGHTS

- Views of the Dam
- Tribunal
- Citizen's Hall
- Façade

DID YOU KNOW?

- The state bought the palace in 1936 for €4.5 million
- The palace rests on 13,659 piles driven 18m (60ft) into the ground
- It is 80m (265ft) long and 56m (125ft) wide
- The bell tower is 51m (119ft) high

INFORMATION

www.koninklijkhuis.nl

✉ Nieuwezijds Voorburgwal 147, Dam

☎ 6204060

🕙 Easter and Jun–end Aug daily 11–5; Sep–mid-Dec and mid-Feb–end May Tue–Thu and Sat–Sun 12.30–5 (but varies depending on state functions; phone for details)

🚊 Tram 1, 2, 4, 5, 6, 9, 13, 14, 16, 17, 24, 25

♿ Good

🍴 Moderate

🔁 Nieuwe Kerk (➤ 39), Amsterdams Historisch Museum (➤ 37), Begijnhof (➤ 36)

Civic pride At the height of the Golden Age, architect Jacob van Campen was commissioned to design Europe's largest and grandest town hall, and its classical design was a startling and progressive departure from the Dutch Renaissance style. The poet Constantijn Huygens called the Stadhuis 'the world's Eighth Wonder' and to this day it remains the city's only secular building on such a grand scale. Note the façade's astonishing wealth of decoration, numerous statues, an elaborate pediment and a huge cupola crowned by a galleon weather vane. During the seven years of construction, a heated argument developed as to whether a tower for the Nieuwe Kerk should have priority over a town hall. This was resolved when the old town hall burned down, and in 1655 the mayor moved into his new building.

Palatial splendour The town hall was transformed into a royal palace in 1808 after Napoleon made his brother Louis King of Holland. Today it serves as an occasional residence for Queen Beatrix, whose principal palace is in The Hague. Inside, be sure to see the Tribunal and the sumptuous Burgerzaal (Citizen's Hall), running the length of the palace, with the eastern and western hemispheres mapped out in marble on the floor. The Tribunal was once the city's main courtroom, and condemned prisoners were taken from here to be hanged publicly on the Dam. The graceful Schepenzaal (Council Chamber), where the city aldermen met, has Rembrandt pupil Ferdinand Bol's painting of *Moses the Lawgiver*.

Nieuwe Kerk

Considering its turbulent history, it is something of a miracle that Holland's magnificent national church has survived. Hearing its organ is a real treat.

Not so new The 'New' Church actually dates from the 15th century, when Amsterdam was growing at such a rate that the 'Old' Church (Oude Kerk, ► 42) was no longer sufficient. Construction started in 1408 but the church was several times destroyed by fire. After the Alteration in 1578 (when Amsterdam officially became Protestant), and a further fire in 1645, the church was rebuilt and reconsecrated in 1648. It has no spire: Following years of debate, the money designated for its construction was spent to complete the neighbouring Stadhuis (Town Hall), which is now the Koninklijk Paleis (► 38). It does have one of the finest of Amsterdam's 42 historic church organs—a Schonat-Hagerbeer organ, dating from 1650–73, with 5,005 pipes and a full-voiced sound that easily fills the church's vast interior.

Famous names At the time of the Alteration, Amsterdam's churches were largely stripped of their treasures, and the Nieuwe Kerk was no exception. The altar space has since been occupied by the tomb of Holland's most valiant naval hero, Admiral Michiel de Ruyter, one of many names from Dutch history, including poets Peter Cornelisz Hooft and Joost van den Vondel, buried here. A window dated 1650 shows the granting of the city's coat of arms by William IV. Another, by Otto Mengelberg to mark her 40th year as queen, shows Wilhelmina at her inauguration in 1898. Dutch monarchs have been inaugurated here, from William I in 1815 to Beatrix in 1980. No longer a place of worship, it hosts exhibitions and organ recitals.

Top: Tomb of Michiel de Ruyter. Above: The Nieuwe Kerk from the Dam

HIGHLIGHTS

- Organ, Hans Schonat and Jacob Hagerbeer (1650–73)
- Organ case, Jacob van Campen (1645)
- Pulpit, Albert Vinckenbrinck (1644)
- Tomb of Admiral de Ruyter, Rombout Verhulst (1681)

INFORMATION

www.nieuwekerk.nl
✉ Dam ☎ 6268168
🕐 Usually daily 10–6 (Thu to 10 during exhibitions)
🍴 Nieuwe Kafé
🚊 Tram 1, 2, 5, 4, 6, 9, 13, 14, 16, 17, 24, 25
♿ Good
🎫 Varies with exhibitions

Bloemenmarkt

Golden sunflowers, deep blue irises, delicately scented roses and row upon row of tulips and tulip bulbs— the barges that serve as stalls for Amsterdam's flower market are ablaze with colour, whatever the season.

HIGHLIGHTS

- De Tuin bulb stall, opposite Singel 502 (➤ 73)
- Van Zoomeren cactus display, opposite Singel 526
- Vazoplant pots and stalls, opposite Singel 514

INFORMATION

- ⊠ Singel (between Muntplein and Koningsplein)
- 🕐 Mon–Sat 9.30–5
- 🚊 Muntplein
- 🚃 Tram 1, 2, 4, 5, 9, 14, 16, 24, 25
- 🛥 Museumboat stop 4
- ♿ Good

Tulipa Whittalli *from Curtis's Botanical Magazine c 1795*

Floating market During the 17th and 18th centuries there were approximately 20 floating markets in Amsterdam, at least two of which gratified the Dutch passion for tulips. Nurserymen would sail up the Amstel from their smallholdings and moor here to sell their wares directly from their boats. Today, the stalls at this, the city's only remaining floating market, are permanently moored—and not all of the sales space is actually afloat. Offering a vast variety of seasonal flowers, plants, pots, shrubs and herbs, they are supplied by the florists of Aalsmeer and the region around Haarlem, at the horticultural heart of Holland. Over 16,000ha (39,540 acres) of the country are devoted to bulb growing.

Tulip mania Tulips were first spotted in Turkey by Dutch diplomats, who brought them back to Holland around 1600. Shortly afterwards, a Leiden botanist discovered ways of changing their shape and colour, and tulip cultivation rapidly became a national obsession. Prices soared, with single bulbs fetching up to €1,360 (an average worker's annual salary was €68). Some were even exchanged for houses, and an abundance of still life paintings was produced to capture prize blooms on canvas. In 1637, the bubble burst, and many people lost entire fortunes. Prices are more realistic today and tulip bulbs are popular souvenirs for tourists. The Bloemenmarkt remains the best place to buy the many varieties.

Rosse Buurt

Amsterdam's Red-Light District, bathed in a lurid red neon glow, and full of gaping tourists, junkies and pickpockets, is one of the city's greatest attractions. Among the sleaziness, everyday life carries on regardless.

Sex for sale Because of the port and its sailor population, sex is, and has long been, big business in Amsterdam. As early as the 15th century, Amsterdam was infamous as a haunt of prostitution, and the lure of the Red-Light District proves irresistible to most visitors to the city today. Crowds clog the narrow alleyways, sex shops, peep shows and suggestively named bars, while bored prostitutes beckon from their pink-lit windows. But there is more to the Red-Light District than sex. 'Normal' people live here, too, and go about their everyday business in what, behind the tawdry façade, is an interesting part of the old city.

Drug central The Red-Light District is also frequented by drug dealers, and here you will find the great majority of Amsterdam's psychedelic, marijuana-selling 'smoking' coffee shops (► 71). The Hash Marihuana Hemp Museum on Oudezijds Achterburgwal is the only museum in Europe tracing the history of hashish and the cannabis plant, and is next to the world's only Cannabis Connoisseurs' Club.

Precautions Watch your wallet, avoid eye contact with any undesirable characters, do not take photographs of prostitutes and avoid poorly lit alleyways. Even though the evening is the liveliest time to visit, it is best not to wander around alone. Stay alert in the Red-Light District and exercise caution in quiet areas at night, or avoid them completely.

DID YOU KNOW?

- Possession of drugs is technically illegal but the authorities tolerate possession of up to 5g (1oz) of soft drugs (cannabis, hashish and marijuana) for personal use
- Drug-dealing is not allowed. 'Smoking' coffee shops have to be licensed
- There are 900 'coffee shops' and 250 cannabis 'grow shops' in Holland, and around 30,000 'home-growers'
- Brothels were legalized in 1990
- Half of Amsterdam's prostitutes are foreign

INFORMATION

- ✉ Borders roughly denoted by Zeedijk (north), Kloveniersburgwal (east), Damstraat (south) and Warmoesstraat (west)
- 🍴 Restaurants, bars, cafés
- 🚉 Centraal Station, Nieuwmarkt
- 🚋 Tram 4, 9, 14, 16, 24, 25
- ↔ Oude Kerk (► 42), Museum Amstelkring (► 43)

Oude Kerk

HIGHLIGHTS

- Great Organ, Vatermüller
- Stained-glass windows, Lambert van Noort (1555)
- Carillon, F. Hemony (1658)

INFORMATION

www.oudekerk.nl
- ✉ Oudekerksplein 1
- ☎ 6258284
- ⏰ Mon–Sat 11–5, Sun 1–5. Closed 1 Jan, 25 Dec
- 🚋 Tram 4, 9, 16, 24, 25
- ♿ Good
- 💶 Moderate
- ↔ Rosse Buurt (➤ 41)
- ❓ Frequent organ recitals and carillon concerts

The 18th-century Great Organ

Surrounded by cafés, bars and sex shops, the Old Church represents an island of spirituality in the Red-Light District. Here brashness and purity rub shoulders.

History Amsterdam's oldest church, dedicated to St. Nicholas, the patron saint of seafarers, was built in 1306 to replace a wooden chapel that probably dated from the late 1200s. Over the centuries the church escaped the great fires that devastated so much of the city, and the imposing basilica you see today dates largely from the 14th century. Its graceful tower, added in 1565–67, contains one of the finest carillons in Holland. In the 16th century Jan Pieters zoon Sweelinck, Holland's best-known composer, was organist here.

Miracle In the 14th century, the Oude Kerk became one of Europe's pilgrimage centres following a miracle: Communion bread regurgitated by a dying man and thrown on the fire would not burn, and the sick man did not die. Thousands of Catholics still take part in the annual *Stille Omgang*, a silent nocturnal procession, but as the Oude Kerk is now Protestant, it no longer follows the ancient pilgrim route to the church, going instead to the Begijnhof.

Sober interior The stark, impressive interior has a triple nave and elaborate vaulting. Three magnificent windows in the Lady Chapel survived the Alteration, as did the finely carved choir stalls. In the 1960s some delicate 14th-century paintings were found behind layers of blue paint in the vaults. The tombstone of Rembrandt's first wife, Saskia van Uylenburg, is still in the church even though poverty drove him to sell her grave plot.

Museum Amstelkring

Not only is this tiny museum one of the city's most surprising, it is also off the beaten tourist track, tucked away in a small, inconspicuous canal house on the edge of the Red-Light District.

Best-kept secret In 1578, when the Roman Catholic city council was replaced by a Protestant one Roman Catholic churches were closed throughout the city. In 1661, while Catholic church services were still forbidden, a wealthy merchant named Jan Hartman built a residence on Oudezijds Voorburgwal, and two adjoining houses in Heintje Hoeckssteeg. He ran a sock shop on the ground floor, lived upstairs, rented out the spare rooms in the buildings behind and cleverly converted the top two storeys of the canal house, and the attics of all three buildings, into a secret Catholic church. Religious freedom only returned with the French occupation of the Netherlands in 1795.

Hidden church This 'schuilkerk' was just one of many clandestine churches that sprang up throughout the city, but it is the only one that has been completely preserved. It was saved from demolition in 1888 by a group of historians called the Amstelkring (Amstel Circle), who nicknamed the church 'Our Dear Lord in the Attic'. To find a three-storey, galleried church at the top of a series of increasingly steep staircases is a surprising experience. Given that there is seating for 200 people, magnificent ecclesiastical statuary, silver, paintings, a collapsible altar and a huge organ, it is hard to believe that the services held here were really secret. Look for the resident priest's tiny hidden bedroom under the stairs, and the confessional on the landing. The rest of the complex has been restored, and provides a taste of domestic life in the 17th century.

HIGHLIGHTS

- Church of 'Our Dear Lord in the Attic'
- Altar painting *The Baptism of Christ,* Jacob de Wit (1716)
- Priest's bedroom
- Confessional
- Drawing room
- Kitchen

DID YOU KNOW?

- The altarpiece is one of three paintings by Jacob de Wit, designed to be interchangeable
- The church is still a consecrated place of worship

HIGHLIGHTS

www.museum amstelkring.nl
- Oudezijds Voorburgwal 40
- 6246604
- Mon–Sat 10–5, Sun, public hols 1–5. Closed 1 Jan, 30 Apr
- Centraal Station
- Tram 4, 9, 16, 24, 25
- Centraal Station
- Museumboat stop 1
- None
- Moderate
- Classical concerts during winter

Top: 'Our Dear Lord in the Attic'

Stedelijk Museum CS

HIGHLIGHTS

- *The Parakeet and the Mermaid*, Matisse (1952–3)
- *The Women of the Revolution*, Kiefer (1986)
- *My Name as Though it were Written on the Surface of the Moon*, Nauman (1986)
- *Sitting Woman with Fish Hat*, Picasso (1942)
- *Beanery*, Kienholz (1965)
- Rietveld furniture collection

INFORMATION

www.stedelijk.nl

✉ Oosterdokskade 3–5. Note that the museum plans to return to its permanent premises at Paulus Potterstraat 13 by mid-2006

☎ 5732911

🕐 Daily 11–5

🚉 Centraal Station

🚋 Tram 1, 2, 4, 5, 6, 9, 13, 16, 17, 24, 25

🚢 Museumboat stop 1

♿ Moderate

🚻 Moderate

↔ Oude Kerk (➤ 42), Museum Amstelkring (➤ 43)

❓ Lectures, films and concerts.

Top: Special exhibitions are a feature of the Stedelijk Museum

One of the world's leading modern art museums. From Henri Matisse to Kazimir Malevich and Piet Mondrian, from Paul Klee to Vasily Kandinsky and Edward Keinholz, this gallery is an essential stop for art enthusiasts.

Controversial The Stedelijk or Municipal Museum, Amsterdam's foremost venue for contemporary art, was founded in 1895. The museum is temporary housed in the former Post Building, in the old harbour area east of Centraal Station (hence the temporary addition of 'CS' to its name) while its regular home is being refurbished and expanded. Its collection of over 25,000 paintings, sculptures, drawings, graphics and photographs contains works by some of the great names of modern art (Van Gogh, Cézanne, Picasso, Monet, Chagall), but the main emphasis is on progressive postwar movements.

House of Museums In 1938 the Stedelijk became Holland's National Museum of Modern Art, but it achieved its worldwide avant-garde reputation in 1945–63, when it was under the dynamic direction of Willem Sandberg. He put much of its existing collection in storage and created a House of Museums in which art, photography, dance, theatre, music and cinema were all represented in innovative shows.

Cutting edge Museum highlights include suprematist paintings by Malevich; works by Mondrian, Gerrit Rietveld and other exponents of the Dutch *De Stijl* school; and a remarkable collection of almost childlike paintings by the *Cobra* movement, founded in defiance of the artistic complacency of postwar Europe, and named after the native cities of its members—Copenhagen, Brussels and Amsterdam.

Museum Willet-Holthuysen

Behind the impressive façade of this beautifully preserved, gracious mansion lies a lavishly decorated, sumptuously furnished home with a delightful garden, a rare luxury in Amsterdam.

Insight Standing on Herengracht, Amsterdam's most elegant canal (➤ 34), this house was built in 1687 for Jacob Hop, a wealthy member of the city council. It changed hands many times and eventually, in 1855, came into the possession of a glass merchant named Pieter Gerard Holthuysen. On his death, it became the home of his daughter Sandra and her husband, the art-collector Abraham Willet, who together built up a valuable collection of glass, silver, ceramics and paintings. The couple bequeathed the house and its contents to the city in 1895, to be used as a museum. For many years it was visited so rarely that people joked that it was the best place for a gentleman to meet his mistress unobserved. However, following extensive restoration in the late 1990s, the museum attracts an ever increasing number of visitors, and provides a rare insight into life in the grand canal-houses in the 17th to 19th centuries.

Luxury and grandeur The rooms are decorated with inlaid wood and lacquered panelling with painted ceilings. Be sure to see the Blue Room, formerly the preserve of the gentlemen of the house, and the 17th-century kitchen, with its original plumbing. Guests would be served tea in the tiny, round Garden Room that, painted in the customary pale green, looks out over an immaculate French-style formal garden, lined with topiary and studded with statues. This is one of the city's few surviving 18th-century gardens—and is a jewel not to be missed.

HIGHLIGHTS

- Blue Room
- Dining Room
- Porcelain and silver collections
- Kitchen
- Garden Room
- Garden

INFORMATION

www.willetholthuysen.nl
- ✉ Herengracht 605
- ☎ 5231822
- ◷ Mon–Fri 10–5, Sat–Sun 11–5. Closed 1 Jan, 30 Apr, 25 Dec
- Ⓜ Waterlooplein
- 🚊 Tram 4, 9, 14
- 🚢 Museumboat stop 3
- ♿ None
- 💶 Moderate
- ↔ Herengracht (➤ 34), Magere Brug (➤ 47), Joods Historisch Museum (➤ 48)

Museum Het Rembrandthuis

HIGHLIGHTS

- *Self-portrait with a Surprised Expression*
- *Five Studies of the Head of Saskia and One of an Older Woman*
- *View of Amsterdam*
- *Christ Shown to the People*

INFORMATION

www.rembrandthuis.nl

- ✉ Jodenbreestraat 4
- ☎ 5200400
- 🕐 Mon–Sat 10–5, Sun, public hols 1–5. Closed 1 Jan
- Ⓜ Nieuwmarkt, Waterlooplein
- 🚋 Tram 9, 14
- 🚢 Museumboat stop 3
- ♿ Few
- 💲 Expensive
- ❓ Brief film of Rembrandt's life

Below: Self-portrait with Saskia *Rembrandt, 1636*

The absence of Rembrandt's own belongings from this intimate house is more than compensated for by its collection of his etchings, which is virtually complete. They are fascinating.

From riches to rags In this red-shuttered canal house, Rembrandt spent the happiest and most successful years of his life, producing many of his most famous paintings and prints here. Though his wife, the wealthy heiress Saskia van Uylenburg, the up-and-coming young artist had been introduced to Amsterdam's patrician class and commissions for portraits had poured in. He had rapidly become an esteemed painter, and bought this large, three-storey house in 1639 as a symbol of his newfound respectability. After Saskia's tragic death, age 30, in 1642 shortly after the birth of their son Titus, Rembrandt's work became unfashionable, and in 1656 he was declared bankrupt. The house and most of his possessions were sold in 1658, although Rembrandt continued to live here until 1660. He died a pauper in 1669 (▶ 32). The house is furnished with period fittings, while most of Rembrandt's works are in a separate wing.

Funny faces It is a strange experience to see 260 of the 280 etchings ascribed to Rembrandt in the very surroundings in which they were created. His achievements in etching were as important as those in his painting, since his mastery in this medium inspired its recognition as an art form for the first time. Four of his copper etching plates are also on display, together with a series of biblical illustrations. Look out for Rembrandt's studies of street figures hung alongside some highly entertaining self-portraits in various guises, and some mirror-images of himself making faces.

Magere Brug

This traditional double-leaf Dutch drawbridge is a city landmark, and one of the most photographed sights in Amsterdam at night, illuminated by strings of enchanting lights.

Skinny sisters Of Amsterdam's 1,200 or so bridges, the wooden 'Skinny Bridge' is, without doubt, the best known. Situated on the Amstel river, it is a 20th-century replica of a 17th-century drawbridge. Tradition has it that, in 1670, a simple footbridge was built by two elderly sisters named *Mager* (meaning skinny), who lived on one side of the Amstel and wanted easy access to their carriage and horses, stabled on the other bank. It seems more likely, however, that the bridge took its name from its narrow girth. In 1772 it was widened and became a double drawbridge, enabling ships of heavy tonnage to sail up the Amstel from the IJ, an inlet of what was then a sea called the Zuider Zee and is today the IJsselmeer, a freshwater lake.

City uproar In 1929 the city council started discussing whether to demolish the old frame, which had rotted. It was to be replaced with an electrically operated bridge. After a huge outcry, the people of Amsterdam voted overwhelmingly to save the original wooden bridge.

Speedy opening The present bridge, made of African azobe wood, was erected in 1969 and its mechanical drive installed in 1994. Every now and then, you can watch the bridge master raising the bridge to let boats through. He then jumps on his bicycle and rides hastily upstream to open the Amstel and Hoge sluice gates, only to mount his bike again, return downstream, and repeat the whole procedure in reverse.

DID YOU KNOW?

- Around 63,000 boats pass under the bridge each year
- Rebuilding in 1969 cost €63,530
- There are 60 drawbridges in Amsterdam; 8 are wooden

INFORMATION

- ✉ At Kerkstraat on the Amstel River
- Ⓜ Waterlooplein
- 🚊 Tram 4
- 🚢 Museumboat stop 3
- ↔ Museum Willet-Holthuysen (▶ 45), Joods Historisch Museum (▶ 48), Hermitage Amsterdam (▶ 58)

Top: The Magere Brug, all lit up at night

Joods Historisch Museum

DID YOU KNOW?

- 1597 First Jew gained Dutch citizenship
- 1602 Judaism first practised openly here
- 1671 The Grote Schul became the first synagogue in Western Europe
- 102,000 of the 140,000-strong Dutch Jewish community were exterminated in World War II
- Restoration of the synagogues cost over €6 million

INFORMATION

www.jhm.nl
- ✉ Jonas Daniël Meijerplein 2–4
- ☎ 6269945
- 🕐 Daily 11–5. Closed Yom Kippur
- 🍴 Café
- Ⓦ Waterlooplein
- 🚃 Tram 9, 14,
- 🚢 Museumboat stop 3
- ♿ Very good 💶 Moderate

Top: The Great Synagogue

A remarkable exhibition devoted to Judaism and the story of Jewish settlement in Amsterdam. The most memorable and poignant part portrays the horrors of the Holocaust.

Reconstruction Located in the heart of what used to be a Jewish neighbourhood, this massive complex of four former synagogues forms the largest and most important Jewish museum outside Israel. The buildings lay in ruins for many years after World War II, but have since been painstakingly reconstructed as a monument to the strength of the Jewish faith and to the suffering of the Jewish people under the Nazis.

Historical exhibits The New Synagogue (1752) gives a lengthy, detailed history of Zionism, with displays of religious artefacts. The Great Synagogue (1671), of more general interest, defines the role of the Jewish community in Amsterdam's trade and industry. Downstairs is a chilling exhibition from the war years and a moving collection by Jewish painters, including a poignant series entitled *Life? or Theatre?* (1940–42) by Charlotte Salomon, who died in Auschwitz aged 26.

The Dockworker The Nazis occupied Amsterdam in May 1940 and immediately began to persecute the Jewish population. In February 1941, 400 Jews were gathered outside the Great Synagogue by the SS, herded into trucks and taken away. This triggered the February Strike, a general strike led by dockers. Though suppressed after only two days, it was Amsterdam's first open revolt against Nazism and gave impetus to the resistance movement. Every 25 February, a ceremony at Andriessen's statue *The Dockworker* commemorates the strike.

Nederlands Scheepvaart Museum

Holland's glorious seafaring history gets due recognition at this museum, which displays with contemporary flair a fine collection of ships, full-size replicas, and models and artefacts.

Admiralty storehouse The vast neoclassical building (1656) that now houses the Maritime Museum was formerly the Dutch Admiralty's central store. Here the United East India Company (VOC) would load their ships prior to the eight-month journey to Jakarta, headquarters of the VOC in Indonesia. In 1973, the arsenal was converted into this museum, which has the largest collection of ships in the world.

Voyages of discovery An ancient dugout, a re-created section of a destroyer, schooners and luxury liners depict Holland's remarkable maritime history. Children can peer through periscopes and operate a radar set, while parents marvel at some 500 magnificent model ships and study the charts, instruments, weapons, maps and globes from the great age of exploration. Don't miss the first-ever sea atlas, the mid-16th century three-masted ship model, or the beautiful royal sloop—the 'golden coach on water'—last used in 1962 for Queen Juliana's silver wedding anniversary.

The *Amsterdam* The highlight of the museum is moored alongside—the *Amsterdam*, a replica of the 18th-century Dutch East Indiaman that sank off the English coast in 1749 during her maiden voyage. A vivid film *Voyage to the East Indies* is shown, and in summer, actors become bawdy 'sailors', firing cannons, swabbing the decks, loading cargo and enacting burials at sea.

HIGHLIGHTS

- The *Amsterdam*
- Royal sloop
- Blaeu's World Atlas (Room 1)
- First printed map of Amsterdam (Room 1)
- Three-masted ship (Room 2)
- Wartime exhibits (Rooms 21–24)

INFORMATION

www. scheepvaartmuseum.nl
- ✉ Kattenburgerplein 1
- ☎ 5232222
- 🕐 Tue–Sun 10–5 (also Mon 10–5, mid-Jun to mid-Sep, and hols). Closed 1 Jan, 30 Apr, 25 Dec. Crew on board *Amsterdam* in summer Mon–Sat 10.30–4.15, Sun 12.30–4.15; winter Tue–Sun 11–3
- 🍴 Restaurant
- 🚌 Bus 22, 32
- ⛴ Museumboat stop 2
- ♿ Very good
- 💰 Expensive
- ↔ Artis Zoo (► 61), Hortus Botanicus (► 60)
- ❓ Souvenir and bookshop, model-boat kit shop Thu and Fri only, multimedia theatre.

Top: The ornate stern of the replica of the Amsterdam

49

Tropenmuseum

INFORMATION

www.kit.nl/tropenmuseum
✉ Linnaeusstraat 2
☎ 5688215; Children's Museum ☎ 5688233
◉ Mon–Sun 10–5; closed 1 Jan, 30 Apr, 5 May, 25 Dec. Children's Museum Wed afternoons, Sat–Sun and Mon–Fri during school hols
🍴 Ekeko restaurant
🚋 Tram 9, 10, 14, 20
♿ Very good
💰 Expensive
↔ Artis Zoo (▶ 61), Hortus Botanicus (▶ 60)
❓ Soeterijn Theater. Shop ☎ 5688233 for further information

Top: Statue of a Hindu goddess in the Tropenmuseum

In the extraordinary Tropical Museum, once a hymn to colonialism, colourful reconstructions of street scenes with sounds, photographs and slide presentations evoke contemporary life in tropical regions.

Foundations In 1859, Frederik Willem van Eeden, a member of the Dutch Society for the Promotion of Industry, was asked to establish a collection of objects from the Dutch colonies 'for the instruction and amusement of the Dutch people'. The collection started with a simple bow, arrows and quiver from Borneo and a lacquer water scoop from Palembang, then expanded at a staggering rate, as did the number of visitors. In the 1920s, to house the collection, the palatial Colonial Institute was constructed and adorned with stone friezes to reflect Holland's imperial achievements. In the 1970s, the emphasis shifted away from the glories of colonialism towards an explanation of Third World problems. Beside the museum is the Oosterpark, a pleasant green space.

Another world The precious collections are not displayed in glass cases, but instead are set out in lifelike settings, amid evocative sounds, photographs and slide presentations, so that you feel as if you've stepped into other continents. Explore a Bombay slum, feel the fabrics in an Arabian souk, have a rest in a Nigerian bar, contemplate in a Hindu temple or listen to the sounds of Latin America in a café. There is also a theatre, the Soeterijn, where visiting performers mount performances of non-Western music, theatre and dance in the evenings. During the day, activities in the children's section (in Dutch only), Kindermuseum TM Junior, give youngsters (aged 6–12) an insight into other cultures.

AMSTERDAM's
best

Canals & Waterways

SUNKEN BOOTY

The canals receive many of the city's unwanted items. More than 100 million L (25 million gal) of sludge and rubbish are removed annually by a fleet of ten municipal boats: six for recovering floating refuse, one for retrieving bikes (about 10,000 a year), using hooks, and three dredgers. Among the so-called treasures they find are stolen wallets, parking meters, cars with failed hand brakes and even an occasional corpse.

AMSTEL

The river is a busy commercial thoroughfare, with barges carrying goods to and from the port. In town, its bustling banks are lined by houseboats, but continue south and you are soon in idylic countryside beyond Amstelpark (► 60).
🚋 Tram 3, 6, 7, 9, 10, 12, 14

AMSTERDAM–RHINE CANAL

This important European waterway stretches from Amsterdam's eastern IJ chanel to the Rhine (Waal) River at Tiel.
🚌 Bus 37, 220, 245

BLAUWBURGWAL

Amsterdam's shortest canal extends between Singel and Herengracht, at Herenstraat.
🚋 Tram 1, 2, 5, 6, 13, 17

BLOEMGRACHT AND EGELANTIERSGRACHT

Narrow canals in the Jordaan, a retreat from the bustle of downtown, lined with colourful small boats.
🚋 Tram 6, 13, 14, 17

BROUWERSGRACHT

Stretching from the Canal Ring into the Jordaan, the Brouwersgracht owes its name to the many breweries established here in the 16th and 17th centuries. Houseboats and the old warehouses that line the canal (once used to store barley, now luxury apartments) make this leafy canal particularly photogenic.
🚇 Centraal Station

The junction of Keizersgracht and Reguliersgracht

GROENBURGWAL

This idyllic, picturesque canal near the
Muziektheater was Monet's favourite.
🚇 Nieuwmarkt

THE IJ

Amsterdam is situated on precariously low-lying
ground at the confluence of the IJ (an inlet of the
IJsselmeer lake) and the Amstel river. During
Amsterdam's heyday in the 17th century,
most maritime activity was centred on the
IJ inlet and along Prins Hendrikkade,
where the old warehouses were crammed
with exotic produce from the East. Since
1876, access to the sea has been via the
North Sea Canal, and the industrial docks
are now to the west. The IJ is busy with
pleasure boats, barges sailing to and from
the port, the free shuttle ferries to
Amsterdam-Noord, the paying ferries that
connect other points along the waterfront
and an occasional warship and cruise liner.
🚇 Centraal Station

*A bridge over the
Keizersgracht*

KEIZERSGRACHT

Together with Prinsengracht and Herengracht, this
broad, elegant canal, built in 1612 and named
Emperor's Canal after Emperor Maximilian I,
completes the Grachtengordel (Canal Ring)—the trio
of concentric central canals, that, intersected by a
series of narrower, radial waterways, make a cobweb
of water across the city. You can skate on it in winter
(if the water freezes, which doesn't always happen).
🚊 Tram 1, 2, 5, 6, 13, 14, 16, 17, 24, 25

LEIDSEGRACHT

One of the most exclusive addresses in town.
🚊 Tram 1, 2, 5, 6, 7, 10

LOOIERSGRACHT

In the 17th century, the main industry in the Jordaan
was tanning, hence the name Tanner's Canal.
🚊 Tram 6, 7, 10

**OUDEZIJDS ACHTERBURGWAL AND
OUDEZIJDS VOORBURGWAL**

In contrast to most of Amsterdam's canals, which are
peaceful and romantic, parts of Oudezijds
Achterburgwal and Oudezijds Voorburgwal are lined
with glaring, neon-lit bars and sex shops. The
southern sections of both are leafier.
🚊 Tram 4, 9, 14, 16, 24, 25

REGULIERSGRACHT

Seven bridges cross the water here in quick
succession. They are best viewed from the water at
night, when they are lit by strings of lights.
🚊 Tram 4, 16, 24, 25

OLD HARBOUR

Many of the installations have
been razed and innovative
modern architecture has been
springing up along the
waterfront. The city's old
harbour has been taken over
by developers, but for a taste
of its former glory, head for
the Scheepvaart Museum
(► 49) in the Eastern Islands,
or to the Western Islands,
where the carefully restored
17th-century warehouses,
cluttered wharfs and nautical
street names like
Zeilmakerstraat (Sailmaker
Street) and Touwslagerstraat
(Rope Factory Street) offer a
glimpse of old Amsterdam.
(✉ north of the railway
between Wester-Kanal and
Westerdoksdijk).

Districts

In the Top 25
16 ROSSE BUURT (► 41)

A typically ornate gable

CHINATOWN
Amsterdam's 7,000-strong Chinese community earns part of its living from the numerous Chinese restaurants around Nieuwmarkt.
🚇 Nieuwmarkt

JODENHOEK
Jewish refugees first came here in the 16th century and settled on cheap, marshy land southeast of Nieuwmarkt and bordered by the Amstel. Almost the entire district was razed to the ground at the end of World War II, leaving only a few synagogues (► 48) and diamond factories as legacy of a once-thriving community.
🚇 Waterlooplein

DE JORDAAN
This popular bohemian quarter with its labyrinth of picturesque canals, narrow streets, trendy shops, cafés and restaurants was once a boggy meadow alongside Prinsengracht. A slum in the 17th century, it later became a more respectable working-class district. The name is believed to have come from the French *jardin*, meaning garden.
🚊 Tram 3, 6, 10, 13, 14, 17

GRACHTENGORDEL (CANAL RING)
The buildings along the web of canals around the medieval city are supported on thousands of wooden piles to stop them from sinking. Constructed as part of a massive 17th-century expansion project, the immaculate patrician mansions along Prinsengracht, Keizersgracht and Herengracht look almost like a toy town in a child's picture book, with their trim brickwork and characterful gables. The best way to enjoy their architectural details is from the water.

DE PIJP
This lively, multicultural area was once one of Amsterdam's most attractive working-class districts outside the Grachtengordel. The bustling Albert Cuypmarkt takes place daily (► 55), and there are several diamond-cutting workshops.
🚊 Tram 4, 16, 24, 25

PLANTAGE
The Plantation became one of Amsterdam's first suburbs in 1848. Before that, this popular and leafy residential area was parkland.
🚊 Tram 9, 14

ZEEDIJK
Once the sea wall of the early maritime settlement and until around 1990 a haunt of sailors and shady characters, this area on the fringe of the Red-Light District is home to several good bars and restaurants.
🚇 Centraal Station 🚊 Tram 1, 2, 4, 5, 6, 9, 13, 16, 17, 24, 25

Markets

In the Top 25

🔢 BLOEMENMARKT (➤ 40)

ALBERT CUYPMARKT
Amsterdam's biggest, best-known and least expensive general market, named after a Dutch landscape artist, attracts some 20,000 bargain hunters on busy days.
✉ Albert Cuypstraat 🕐 Mon–Sat 10–5 🚊 Tram 4, 16, 24, 25

BEVERWIJKSE BAZAAR
This huge indoor flea market 20km (12.5 miles) northwest of Amsterdam (reputedly Europe's largest) has an Eastern Market overflowing with oriental merchandise.
✉ Industrieterrein De Pijp, Buitenland 30, Beverwijk 🕐 Sat 7–5, Sun (Eastern Market only) 8–6 🚉 Beverwijk-Oost

NOORDERMARKT MARKETS
For a taste of the Jordaan district, head for the lively square surrounding the Noorderkerk. On Monday morning visit the Lapjesmarkt textile and second-hand clothing market, and on Saturday try the Boerenmarkt for organically grown fresh produce, crafts and birds.
✉ Noordermarkt 🕐 Mon–Fri 9–1, Sat 9–4 🚊 Tram 1, 2, 5, 6, 13, 17

OUDEMANHUISPOORT
Antiquarian bookstalls in an
✉ Oudemanhuispoort
🕐 Mon–Fri 11–4 🚊 Tram 4, 9, 14, 16, 24, 25

POSTZEGELMARKT
A specialist market for stamps, coins and medals.
✉ Nieuwezijds Voorburgwal 280
🕐 Wed, Sat 1–4 🚊 Tram 1, 2, 5

ROMMELMARKT
Rommel means rummaging. Bric-a-brac is your cue to the style of the place.
✉ Looiersgracht 38 🕐 Daily 11–5 🚊 Tram 7, 10

WATERLOOPLEIN FLEA MARKET
Amsterdam's liveliest market, full of funky clothes, curiosities and 'antique' junk.
✉ Waterlooplein 🕐 Mon–Sat 9–5 🚇 Waterlooplein

MARKETS
Amsterdam resembles a collection of villages, each having its own local market. The daily markets at Ten Katestraat (Kinkerstraat) and Dapperstraat are good for fruit and vegetables, and there is a flower market at Amstelveld every Monday morning. Sunday art markets are held at Spui from March until Christmas and at Thorbeckeplein from mid-March until November, while you may find a bargain at the Nieuwmarkt antiques market on Sundays in summer.

Albert Cuypmarkt

Bridges, Buildings & Monuments

BRIDGES

Amsterdam has 1,281 bridges. The majority are single or triple-arched hump-backed bridges made of brick and stone with simple cast-iron railings. The oldest bridge is the Torensluis (1648) and the best example of a traditional Dutch drawbridge is the Magere Brug (Skinny Bridge ► 47). The cast-iron Blauwbrug (Blue Bridge, 1874) is one of the most elegant, while the 21st-century, long and graceful Javabrug, which connects the new developments east of Centraal Station to the redeveloped Java Island, is among the most modern.

Rokin 99, a modern interpretation of a canalside house

BEURS VAN BERLAGE

Designed by Hendrik Petrus Berlage and now hailed as an early modernist masterpiece, the former stock exchange provoked outrage when it opened in 1903. It is now a concert hall (► 80).
✉ Beursplein 1 ☎ 6240141 🕐 Museum Tue–Sun 11–5 🚋 Tram 4, 9, 14, 16, 24, 25

CENTRAAL STATION

Many visitors get their first glimpse of Amsterdam's architectural wonders at P. J. H. Cuypers' vast Dutch neo-Renaissance station (1889), standing with its back to the IJ harbour.
✉ Stationsplein ☎ 5578400 🚋 Centraal Station

CONCERTGEBOUW

The orchestra and main concert hall of this elaborate neoclassical building have been renowned worldwide ever since the inaugural concert in 1888.
✉ Concertgebouwplein 2–6 ☎ 6718345 🕐 Box office daily 10–7
🚋 Tram 3, 5, 12, 16, 24

ENTREPOTDOK

The old warehouses at Entrepotdok have been converted into offices and apartments.
✉ Entrepotdok 🚌 Bus 22

GREENPEACE HEADQUARTERS

This pragmatic city seems an appropriate home for the Greenpeace world headquarters, in a remarkable *Jugendstil* (art-nouveau) building dating from 1905.
✉ Keizersgracht 174 ☎ 4223344 🚋 Tram 6, 13, 14, 17

KERWIN DUINMEYER MONUMENT

Kerwin, a 15-year-old black youth, was stabbed to death in Amsterdam in 1983. It was the first time since World War II that someone had been killed in the city because of race. His statue stands in the Vondelpark as a symbol of opposition to racism.
✉ Vondelpark (Jacob Obrechtstraat exit)
🚋 Tram 1, 2, 3, 5, 12

'T LIEVERDJE

In the 1960s this little bronze statue of a boy, which stands so innocently in the middle of the square, became a symbol of the *Provo* movement, and rallying point of frequent anti-establishment demonstrations. The name means 'Little Rascal'.

✉ Spui
🚋 Tram 1, 2, 5

MUNTTOREN

The tower of the former Mint was part of the southern gateway to the medieval city.

✉ Muntplein 🚋 Tram 4, 9, 14, 16, 24, 25

MUZIEKTHEATER

Amsterdam's theatre for opera and dance is known as the false teeth because of its white marble panelling and red brick roof. The complex includes the uninspiring buildings of the new town hall (Stadhuis). The design caused great controversy when it was built in 1986, sparking riots during its construction.

✉ Waterlooplein 22
☎ 6255455
Ⓜ Waterlooplein

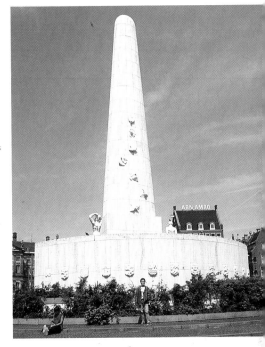

Nationaal Monument on the Dam, in memory of World War II victims

NATIONAAL MONUMENT

The 23-m (75-ft) War Memorial obelisk on the Dam contains soil from the then 11 Dutch provinces and the colonies. Every year on 4 May the Queen lays a wreath here.

✉ Dam 🚋 Tram 4, 9, 14, 16, 24, 25

SCHEEPVAARTHUIS

The peculiarly tapered Maritime House, encrusted with marine decoration, suggests the bow of an approaching ship. Commissioned by seven shipping companies in 1912, it represents one of the most impressive examples of the architecture of the Amsterdam School.

✉ Prins Hendrikkade 108–111 🚌 Bus 22, 32

SCHREIERSTOREN

The Weeping Tower was where tearful wives and girlfriends waved farewell to their seafaring menfolk. They had good reason to weep: Sailing-ship voyages took up to four years and many sailors died.

✉ Prins Hendrikkade 94–95 Ⓜ Centraal Station

HOMOMONUMENT

One of the city's more arresting sculptures is the *Homomonument* (1987) by Dutch artist Karin Daan, on the corner of Westermarkt and Keizersgracht. Consisting of three pink, granite triangles, the sign homosexuals were forced to wear during the Nazi occupation, it commemorates all those who have been persecuted because of their homosexuality.

57

Museums & Galleries

CANAL-HOUSE MUSEUMS

The grand 17th-century canal house Museum van Loon (✉ Keizersgracht 672) has an impressive family portrait gallery. The Theatermuseum (✉ Herengracht 168) and the Bijbels Museum (Bible Museum) (✉ Herengracht 366), with its religious artefacts, are also in beautiful houses whose interiors alone warrant a visit.

A mug of Heineken

AMSTERDAM PASS

In addition to free admission to about 20 museums and attractions, the Amsterdam Pass affords discounted admission to others, reductions on some restaurant and shop bills, a free canal boat tour and reduced fares on the Museumboat and the Canal Bus, plus free use of public transport in the heart of the city for the lifetime of the pass.

In the Top 25

🔢 **AMSTERDAMS HISTORISCH MUSEUM** (➤ 37)
🔢 **ANNE FRANKHUIS** (➤ 33)
🔢 **FILM MUSEUM (VONDELPARK)** (➤ 26)
🔢 **HASH MARIHUANA HEMP MUSEUM** (➤ 41)
🔢 **JOODS HISTORISCH MUSEUM** (➤ 48)
🔢 **MUSEUM AMSTELKRING** (➤ 43)
🔢 **MUSEUM HET REMBRANDTHUIS** (➤ 46)
🔢 **MUSEUM WILLET-HOLTHUYSEN** (➤ 45)
🔢 **NEDERLANDS SCHEEPVAART MUSEUM** (➤ 49)
🔢 **RIJKSMUSEUM** (➤ 28)
🔢 **STEDELIJK MUSEUM CS** (➤ 44)
🔢 **TROPENMUSEUM** (➤ 50)
🔢 **VAN GOGH MUSEUM** (➤ 27)
🔢 **WOONBOOTMUSEUM** (➤ 30)

HEINEKEN EXPERIENCE

An interactive introduction to the world of Heineken beer—followed by free tastings.
✉ Stadhouderskade 78 ☎ 5239666 🕐 Tue–Sun 10–6; last admissions at 5. Closed 1 Jan, 25 Dec 🚃 Tram 4, 6, 7, 10, 16, 24, 25 ♿ Few (phone in advance) 💶 Expensive ❓ No under 18s

HERMITAGE AMSTERDAM

Opened in 2004 in the 17th-century Amstelhof complex, this 'branch' of St. Petersburg's Hermitage Museum won't be fully operational until 2007. The first phase has changing exhibitions taken from the Russian parent's collection of art, fine art and crafts.
✉ Neerlandia Building, Amstelhof, Nieuwe Herengracht 14 ☎ 5308755 🕐 Daily 10–5 🚇 Waterlooplein 🚢 Museumboat stop 3 🚃 9, 14 ♿ Good 💶 Moderate

STEDELIJK MUSEUM BUREAU AMSTERDAM

When the modern art in the Stedelijk Museum (➤ 44) isn't latest-thing enough, try out the ultra cutting-edge works by local artists at this Jordaan satellite gallery.
✉ Rozenstraat 59 ☎ 4220471 🕐 Tue–Sun 11–5. Closed 1 Jan, 30 Apr, 25 Dec 🚃 6, 13, 14, 17 ♿ Moderate 💶 Free

VERZETSMUSEM (RESISTANCE MUSEUM)

Rare wartime memorabilia and a fascinating summary of the Dutch resistance during World War II.
✉ Plantage Kerklaan 61a ☎ 6202535 🕐 Tue–Fri 10–5, Sat–Sun noon–5. Closed 1 Jan, 30 Apr, 25 Dec 🚃 Tram 6, 7, 9, 14 ♿ Good 💶 Moderate

WERF 'T KROMHOUT MUSEUM

Located at one of the city's few remaining working shipyards, this museum documents the development of the Eastern Islands shipbuilding industry.
✉ Hoogte Kadijk 147 ☎ 6276777 🕐 Tue 10–3 🚌 Bus 22, 32 ♿ Few 💶 Inexpensive

Places of Worship

AMSTELKERK

Squat and wooden, this Calvinist church (1670) was originally meant to be a temporary structure while funds were raised for a larger building elsewhere.
✉ Amstelveld ☎ 6238138 🕐 Closed to public except during 10.30am Sun service 🚊 Tram 4

FRANCISCUS XAVERIUSKERK

This splendid neo-Gothic church is often dubbed De Krijtberg (Chalk Hill), because it is built on the site of a former chalk merchant's house.
✉ Singel 442–448 ☎ 6231923 🕐 Services only 🚊 Tram 1, 2, 5

NOORDERKERK

An austere church, the first in Amsterdam to be constructed in the shape of a Greek cross. It was built in 1620–23 for the Protestant workers in the Jordaan district, and is still well attended.
✉ Noordermarkt 44–48 ☎ 6266436 🕐 Sat 11–1, Mon 10.30–1 and services 🚊 Tram 1, 2, 5, 6, 13, 14, 17

PORTUGEES-ISRAËLIETISCHE SYNAGOGE

Holland's finest synagogue, one of the first of any size in Western Europe. It is remarkable that this imposing building escaped destruction in World War II.
✉ Mr Visserplein 3 ☎ 6245351 🕐 Sun–Fri 10–4 and service on Sat at 9am. Closed Jewish holidays, Sun 10–noon 🚇 Waterlooplein 🚢 Museumboat stop 3 💷 Inexpensive

SINT-NICOLAASKERK

Amsterdam's main Roman Catholic church (1888) and one of many Dutch churches named after St. Nicholas, the patron saint of sailors. St. Nicholas is also *Sinterklaas* (see panel). ✉ Prins Hendrikkade 73 ☎ 6844803 🕐 Mon–Sat 11–4 and services 🚊 Tram 1, 2, 4, 5, 6, 9, 13, 16, 17, 24, 25

ZUIDERKERK

Holland's first Protestant church (1614) and indisputably one of the city's most beautiful. Its designer, Hendrick de Keyser, lies buried within. The distinctive 80-m (265-ft) high tower affords spectacular views of the Nieuwmarkt district (closed for safety renovations at time of writing).
✉ Zuiderkerkhof 72 ☎ 6222962 🕐 Mon–Wed, Fri noon–5, Thu noon–8 🚇 Nieuwmarkt

Zuiderkerk

SINTERKLAAS

St. Nicholas, or *Sinterklaas*, pays an early visit to the city each year on the third Saturday of November. Accompanied by *Zwarte Piet* (Black Peter), he arrives by boat near Sint-Nicolaaskerk and distributes gingerbread to children, then receives the keys to the city from the mayor on the Dam. On 5 December (*Sinterklaasavond* or *Pakjesavond*) he comes during the night with sacks of presents for the sleeping children.

59

Parks & Gardens

HORTUS BOTANICUS

Laid out in 1682, the botanical gardens were originally sponsored by the Vereenigde Oost-Indische Compagnie (VOC) whose members brought back plants and seeds from all corners of the earth, to be grown and studied by doctors and apothecaries here. One such plant, a coffee tree given to Louis XIV of France and cultivated in his American colonies, was the ancestor of the Brazilian coffee plantations. Likewise, the production of palm oil in Indonesia is due to plants initially cultivated here.

Vondelpark

AMSTELPARK

A formal rose garden and a rhododendron valley are two of the seasonal spectacles at this magnificent park, created in 1972 for an international horticultural exhibition. It also offers pony rides, miniature golf, a children's farm, the Rieker windmill (➤ 62) and other attractions. There is a walk for blind people, and in summer you can tour the park in a miniature train.
🕓 Dawn–dusk 🍴 Restaurant and café 🚌 Bus 68, 69, 148, 169

AMSTERDAMSE BOS

Amsterdam's largest park was built on the polders outside the city in the 1930s as part of a job creation scheme. It is a popular family destination on weekends whatever the season. In winter, there is tobogganing and skating, in summer swimming, sailing and biking. A leisurely tram ride can be taken through the park in colourful antique cars acquired from various European cities.
✉ Amstelveen 🕓 24 hours 🍴 Open-air pancake restaurant and café 🚌 Bus 170, 171, 172

HORTUS BOTANICUS

With more than 8,000 plant species, Amsterdam's oldest botanical garden (founded in 1638 and established here in 1682) boasts one of the largest collections in the world. It has spectacular tropical greenhouses, a medicinal herb garden orchid nursery and a monumental cycad that, at 400 years old, is reputed to be the world's oldest potted plant (➤ panel).
✉ Plantage Middenlaan 2a
☎ 6259021 🕓 Apr–end Sep Mon–Fri 9–5, Sat–Sun 11–5; Oct–end Mar Mon–Fri 9–4, Sat–Sun 11–4 🍴 Café 🚋 Tram 9, 14 ♿ Good ✋ Moderate

SARPHATIPARK

Enjoy a picnic bought at nearby Albert Cuypmarkt (➤ 55) in this tiny green oasis dedicated to the 19th-century Jewish doctor and city benefactor, Samuel Sarphati.
🕓 9–dusk 🚋 Tram 3, 4, 25

For Children

In the Top 25

ARTIS ZOO (NATURA ARTIS MAGISTRA)

As well as animals, the complex includes museums, an aquarium and the Planetarium (hourly shows). A great day out but it can get crowded.

✉ Plantage Kerklaan 38–40 ☎ 5233400; www.artis.nl 🕐 6 Apr–end Oct daily 9–5 🍴 Restaurant and café 🚋 Tram 7, 9, 14. Artis Express boat from Centraal Station ♿ Good 💶 Expensive

CIRCUS ELLEBOOG

Learn tightrope walking, juggling and other circus skills at the Elleboog Circus. You need to book.

✉ Passeerdersgracht 32 ☎ 6269370 🕐 Times vary, phone for details 🚋 Tram 6, 7, 10 ♿ Good 💶 Expensive

DE KRAKELING THEATER

Mime and puppet shows, for under-12s, and over-12s.

✉ Nieuwe Passeerdersstraat 1 ☎ 6245124 🕐 Shows Thu–Sat 8pm, Sun, Wed 2pm 🚋 Tram 7, 10 ♿ Good 💶 Moderate

KINDERKOOKKAFÉ

A children's restaurant where children between five and twelve can cook, then serve or eat at mini-tables.

✉ Oudezijds Achterburgwal 193 ☎ 6253257 🕐 Sat cooking 3.30–6, dinner 6–8 (age 8 plus); Sun cooking 2.30–5, high tea 5–6 (age 5 plus); Mon–Fri 1–3 🚇 Nieuwmarkt 💶 Expensive

KINDERBOERDERIJ DE PIJP

A farm especially for children, south of the of the city.

✉ Lizzy Ansinghstraat 82 ☎ 6648303 🕐 Mon–Fri 11–5, Sat–Sun 1–5 🚋 Tram 24, 25 ♿ Few 💶 Free

MADAME TUSSAUD'S

Wax models of Rembrandt, Van Gogh, Pavarotti, Schwarzenegger and other characters from the 17th century to the present day, and an amazing 5-m (16-ft) giant clothed in windmills and tulips.

✉ Dam 20 ☎ 5221010 🕐 Sep–end Jun daily 10–6.30 (closed 30 Apr); Jul–end Aug 9.30–8.30 🚋 Tram 4, 9, 14, 16, 24, 25 ♿ Good 💶 Very expensive

NEMO

Children will enjoy learning at this impressive hands-on, interactive museum of modern technology.

✉ Oosterdok 2 ☎ 0900/9191100 🕐 Jul–end Aug daily 10–5; Sep–end Jun Tue–Sun 10–5 (open daily during hols 10–5). Closed 1 Jan, 30 Apr, 25 Dec 🍴 Café 🚌 Bus 22, 32 ♿ Very good 💶 Expensive

OUT OF TOWN

Ask the VVV for details on making excursions to Volendam, where a few villagers still wear traditional costume; the windmill village of Zaanse Schans; to the IJsselmeer (formerly the Zuiderzee), for the open-air Zuidzeemuseum, a reconstructed village at Enkhuizen, or to one of Holland's many theme parks, such as the enchanted forest of De Efteling at Kaatsheuvel or the Duinrell water park at Wassenaar, near The Hague.

PUNCH & JUDY

From mid-April until the end of September there are free Punch and Judy performances on Wed 1–5 on the Dam.

Owl statue at the zoo

Windmills

Amsterdam's most central windmill has been converted into a bar

D'ADMIRAAL

Built in 1792 to grind chalk but now unused.
✉ Noordhollands Kanaaldijk, near Jan Thoméepad, Amsterdam-Noord
🚌 Bus 29, 34, 36, 37

DE BLOEM

This old grain mill, built in 1768, resembles a giant pepper shaker.
✉ Haarlemmerweg, at Nieuwpoortkade
🚌 Bus 18

DE GOOIER (FUNENMOLEN)

Amsterdam's most central mill (1725) was the first grain mill in Holland to use the streamlined sails that became ubiquitous. Built on a brick base, with an octagonal body and a thatched wooden frame, it has been converted into a small brewery and bar, but its massive sails still occasionally creak into action.
✉ Funenkade 🚋 Tram 10; bus 22, 32

DE RIEKER

The finest windmill in Amsterdam was built in 1636 to drain the Rieker polder, and is situated at the southern tip of the Amstelpark. This was one of Rembrandt's favourite painting locations—there is a statue near by his memory. The windmill has been beautifully preserved and is now a private home.
✉ Amsteldijk, near De Borcht 🚌 Bus 148

NATIONAL WINDMILL DAY

Windmills have been a feature of the Dutch landscape since the 13th century. Much of the Netherlands lies below sea level, and windmills were used to drain the land and extend the shoreline, creating the fertile farmland called *polder*. Some 950 survive, and on National Windmill Day (the second Saturday in May), many turn their sails and are open to the public.

1100 ROE

This old smock mill, shaped like a peasant's smock, was one of a '*gang*' of water mills that once drained the polders. It stands 1,100 roes from the city's outer canal. The word *roe* means both the flat part of a sail that had to be set or reefed according to wind strength, and a unit of measurement (about 28cm/1ft) used to calculate the distance from the city's hub.
✉ Herman Bonpad, Sportpark Ookmeer 🚌 Bus 19, 23

1200 ROE

This early 17th-century post mill, with its impressive platform and revolving cap, was built to help drain the polders.
✉ Haarlemmerweg, near Willem Molengraaffstraat 🚌 Bus 85

AMSTERDAM
where to...

63

Dutch Restaurants

OPENING TIMES AND PRICES

The restaurants listed on pages 64–71 are all open for lunch and dinner daily unless otherwise stated. They are divided into three price categories. For a main dish, expect to pay:

€€€ over €30
€€ €15 to €30
€ up to €15

DUTCH TREATS

Numerous restaurants in the city provide a taste of authentic Dutch cuisine. The most delicious dishes include thick split-pea soup (*erwtensoep*), meaty stews (*stamppot*), smoked eel (*gerookte paling*), raw herring (*haring*), sweet and savoury pancakes (*pannekoeken*), waffles (*stroopwafels*) and cheeses. Look out for the special 'Neerlands Dis' sign (a red, white and blue soup tureen), which indicates restaurants commended by this organization for their top-quality traditional Dutch cuisine.

A modern trend is towards 'New Dutch' cuisine. Traditional dishes are prepared with a lighter touch and presented with greater sophistication, using fresh seasonal products and an adventurous mix of herbs and spices.

DE BLONDE HOLLANDER (€)

Generous portions of wholesome and modestly priced fare in a lively bistro setting.

✉ Leidsekruisstraat 28, Grachtengordel ☎ 6233014 🕔 Dinner only 🚊 Tram 1, 2, 5, 6, 7, 10

DORRIUS (€€€)

A sophisticated take on the rustic Dutch style. Sample the pike and salted cod traditional delicacies, or the cheese soufflé.

✉ Crowne Plaza Hotel, Nieuwezijds Voorburgwal 5, Centrum ☎ 4202224 🚊 Tram 1, 2, 5, 6, 13, 17

DE GROENE LANTAARN (€€)

This tiny restaurant, located on a quiet leafy canal, specializes in Gouda fondues.

✉ Bloemgracht 47, Jordaan ☎ 6202088 🚊 Tram 6, 13, 14, 17

HAESJE CLAES (€€)

Dutch cuisine at its best, served in a warren of small, panelled dining rooms in a building dating from the 16th-century.

✉ Spuistraat 275, Centrum ☎ 6249998 🚊 Tram 1, 2, 5

KEUKEN VAN 1870 (€)

This onetime soup kitchen, renovated and a shade gentrified, serves up wholesome and hearty Dutch fare for a modest price.

✉ Spuistraat 4, Centrum ☎ 6204018 🕔 Dinner only 🚊 Tram 1, 2, 5, 6, 13, 17

MOEDER'S POT (€)

No frills food served at communal tables; chunky soups, casseroles, mussels, chicken and ham. No credit cards.

✉ Vinkenstraat 119 ☎ 6237643 🕔 Mon–Sat 5–9.30 🚊 Tram 10, 22

POET DE LEEUW (€–€€)

Steaks, steaks and yet more steaks are the house speciality at this atmospheric old place, but there is some room on the menu for traditional dishes.

✉ Noorderstraat 11, Grachtengordel ☎ 6237181 🚊 Tram 16, 24, 25

DE POORT (€€)

Since 1870, this famous restaurant has sold more than 6 million numbered steaks. Every thousandth one comes with a free bottle of house wine.

✉ Hotel Die Port van Cleve, Nieuwezijds Voorburgwal 176, Centrum ✉ 6240047 🚊 Tram 1, 2, 5, 6, 13, 17

DE ROODE LEEUW (€€)

The brasserie-style Red Lion serves up good stews and sauerkraut dishes.

✉ Hotel Amsterdam, Damrak 93–94, Centrum ☎ 5550666 🕔 10am–11pm, last orders 9.30pm 🚊 Tram 4, 9, 14, 16, 24, 25

D'VIJFF VLIEGHEN (€€€)

The menu in the Five Flies in five 17th-century houses has an impressive collection of 'New Dutch' dishes.

✉ Spuistraat 294–302, Centrum ☎ 6248369 🕔 Dinner only 🚊 Tram 1, 2, 5

Elegant Dining

DE BELHAMEL (€€)

Art nouveau and classical music set the tone for polished Continental cuisine in an intimate, often crowded setting with a superb canal view.
✉ Brouwersgracht 60, Jordaan ☎ 6221095 ⏰ Dinner only 🚊 Tram 1, 2, 5, 6, 13, 17

BORDEWIJK (€€€)

Mediterranean and Asian touches, and a spare, black-and-white interior, add zest to French dishes.
✉ Noordermarkt 7, Jordaan ☎ 6243899 ⏰ Tue–Sun dinner only
🚊 Tram 1, 2, 5, 6, 13, 17

CAFÉ ROUX (€€)

Fine French cuisine in an art-nouveau setting, overlooked by a Karel Appel mural.
✉ Grand Hotel, Oudezijds Voorburgwal 197, Centrum ☎ 5553111 ⏰ Nieuwmarkt

CHRISTOPHE (€€€)

Chef Jean-Christophe Royer combines French style and US experience to great effect in his chic canalside restaurant.
✉ Leliegracht 46, Jordaan ☎ 6250807 ⏰ Mon–Sat dinner only 🚊 Tram 6, 13, 14, 17, 20

LE CIEL BLEU (€€€)

The height of stylish French cuisine on the Okura Hotel's 23rd floor.
✉ Ferdinand Bolstraat 333, Nieuw Zuid ☎ 6787450 ⏰ Dinner and Sun brunch 🚊 Tram 12, 25

LE GARAGE (€€€)

French regional cuisine at its best at this trendy brasserie in a converted garage near Vondelpark.
✉ Ruysdaelstraat 54–56, Oud Zuid ☎ 6797176 ⏰ Dinner daily, lunch Mon–Fri 🚊 Tram 3, 5, 12, 16, 24

DE GOUDEN REAEL (€€€)

French restaurant in a 17th-century dockside building with a romantic waterside terrace.
✉ Zandhoek 14, Westerdok ☎ 6233883 ⏰ Closed Sun 🚊 Tram 3; bus 35

LA RIVE (€€€)

In Amsterdam's most expensive hotel chef Edwin Katz produces excellent regional French cooking.
✉ Amstel Hotel, Prof Tulpplein 1 ☎ 5203264 ⏰ Closed Sat, Sun and lunch Mon 🚊 Tram 6, 7, 10

DE SILVEREN SPIEGEL (€€€)

An exquisite classic menu, complemented by one of the city's best wine lists, in a superbly restored 1614 house. Fish is the house speciality.
✉ Kattengat 4–6, Centrum ☎ 6246589 ⏰ Dinner only; closed Sun except for reserved parties 🚊 Tram 1, 2, 5, 6, 13, 17

HET TUYNHUIS (€€)

Sophisticated French, Portuguese and Dutch cuisine in a converted coach house and garden.
✉ Reguliersdwarsstraat 28, Grachtengordel ☎ 6276603 ⏰ Closed Sat and Sun lunch 🚊 Tram 4, 9, 14, 16, 24, 25

TIPPING

Most restaurant windows display menus giving the price of individual dishes including BTW (value-added tax) and a 15 per cent service charge. Nevertheless, most Amsterdammers leave a small tip or round up the bill (check). This tip should be left as change rather than included on a credit-card payment.

Indonesian Restaurants

A HEARTY MEAL

When the Dutch took over the Spice Islands of the East Indies in the 17th century, they got more than spices out of their new colony. They developed a taste for the exotic local cuisine that survived Indonesian independence and gives Amsterdam today an abundance of *Indonesisch* restaurants.

First-timers to an Indonesian restaurant should order a *rijsttafel*, which includes rice and a complete range of other dishes: *ayam* (chicken), *ikam* (fish), *telor* (egg), *rendang* (beef), *krupuk* (shrimp crackers), shredded coconut and sweet-and-sour vegetables. The *rijsttafel* ('rice table') originally referred to the long list of ingredients required to prepare such a feast. It originated in early colonial days among hungry Dutch planters who, not satisfied by the basic Indonesian meal of rice and vegetables accompanied by meat or fish, continually added other dishes. Thus the *rijsttafel* was born, a meal that ranges from a 6- to 10-item mini-*rijsttafel* to a 20- to 30-dish feast.

ANEKA RASA (€€)

This airy modern restaurant offers numerous vegetarian dishes including an all-vegetarian *rijsttafel*.

✉ Warmoesstraat 25–29, Centrum ☎ 6261560 🕐 Dinner only 🚇 Centraal Station

BOJO (€€)

Popular late-night eatery serving huge portions of rice and noodle dishes and delicious satays. Good size portions, and plenty of vegetarian choices too.

✉ Lange Leids-edwarsstraat 51, Grachtengordel ☎ 6227434 🕐 Mon–Fri dinner, Sat–Sun lunch, dinner 🚊 Tram 1, 2, 5, 6, 7, 10

INDRAPURA (€€)

A popular colonial-style restaurant. Tell the waiter how hot and spicy you want your dishes to be.

✉ Rembrandtplein 40-42, Grachtengordel ☎ 6237329 🕐 Dinner only 🚊 Tram 4, 9, 14

KANTJIL & DE TIJGER (€€)

Modern decor and spicy, imaginative Javanese cuisine. Try the delicious *Nasi Rames*, a mini-*rijsttafel* on one plate.

✉ Spuistraat 291, Centrum ☎ 6200994 🕐 Dinner only 🚊 Tram 1, 2, 5

ORIENT (€€)

This dark, opulent restaurant specializes in *rijsttafels*, with more than 20 different sorts, three of them vegetarian, and an extensive buffet on Wednesdays. A good introduction to Indonesian flavours.

✉ Van Baerlestraat 21, Oud Zuid ☎ 6734958 🕐 Dinner only 🚊 Tram 2, 3, 5, 12

SAHID JAYA (€€)

The shady courtyard garden is especially nice in summer.

✉ Reguliersdwarsstraat 26, Grachtengordel 26 ☎ 6263727 🚊 Tram 1, 2, 5

SAMA SEBO (€€)

Rush mats and batik typify this Balinese setting where you can select from the menu to create your own *rijsttafel*.

✉ P C Hooftstraat 27, Oud Zuid ☎ 6628146 🕐 Closed Sun 🚊 Tram 2, 5

SARANG MAS (€€)

Modern surroundings counterpoint traditional cuisine.

✉ Damrak 44, Centrum ☎ 6222105 🕐 Daily 11.30am–11pm 🚊 Tram 4, 9, 14, 16, 24, 25

SUKASARI (€)

Colourful batik tablecloths, closely packed tables, generous portions.

✉ Damstraat 26-28, Centrum ☎ 6240092 🕐 Tue–Sat dinner, Mon lunch 🚊 Tram 4, 9, 14, 16, 24, 25

TEMPO DOELOE (€€)

One of Amsterdam's best Indonesian restaurants, notable for its western interior, exotic flowers and some of the hottest dishes in town.

✉ Utrechtsestraat 75, Grachtengordel ☎ 6256718 🕐 Dinner only 🚊 Tram 4

Fish & Vegetarian Restaurants

ALBATROS (€€–€€€)

Eschews the fancy demeanour affected by many seafood eateries, preferring to rely on its homey neighbourhood style, and great-tasting seafood.

✉ Westerstraat 264, Jordaan
☎ 6279932 🚊 Tram 3, 10

BODEGA KEYSER (€€)

An Amsterdam institution, just re-opened after a long period of refurbishment, next door to the Concertgebouw, specializing in fish and Dutch dishes.

✉ Van Baerlestraat 96, Oud Zuid ☎ 6711441 🕐 Mon–Sat 9am–midnight, Sun 11am–midnight 🚊 Tram 2, 3, 5, 12, 16

DE OESTERBAR (€€)

The seasonal delights of this elegant fish restaurant include herring in May, mussels in June and delicate Zeeland oysters throughout the summer.

✉ Leidseplein 10, Grachtengordel ☎ 6232988
🕐 Daily noon–midnight
🚊 Tram 1, 2, 5, 6, 7, 10

LE PECHEUR (€€€)

A smart fish-bistro with a secluded garden. Outstanding fresh oysters, caviar, sashimi and lobster.

✉ Reguliersdwarsstraat 32, Grachtengordel ☎ 6243121
🕐 Closed Sat lunch and all day Sun 🚊 Tram 1, 2, 5

VIS AAN DE SCHELDE (€€)

This popular fish restaurant boasts an electic menu of fish dishes from around the world. Dine in the art-deco interior or out on the patio.

✉ Scheldeplein 4, Rivierbuurt

☎ 6751583 🕐 Dinner only
🚊 Tram 12, 25

VISRESTAURANT JULIA (€)

Julia's fish platter, with ten kinds of fish, baked, barbecued and grilled, draws people from all over.

✉ Amstelveenseweg 160
☎ 6795394 🕐 Tue–Sun dinner only 🚌 Bus 146, 147, 170, 171, 172

VEGETARIAN

DE BOLHOED (€)

A trendy restaurant on the edge of the Jordaan, with vegetarian pâtés, salads and hearty vegan dishes.

✉ Prinsengracht 60-62, Grachtengordel ☎ 6261803
🚊 Tram 6, 13, 14, 17

GOLDEN TEMPLE (€)

An imaginative menu of Indian, Mexican and Middle Eastern dishes.

✉ Utrechtsestraat 126, Grachtengordel ☎ 6268560
🕐 Dinner only 🚊 Tram 4

HEMELSE MODDER (€€)

Sophisticated main courses and delicious desserts.

✉ Oude Waal 11, Centrum
☎ 6243203 🕐 Tue–Sun dinner only 6–10 (last admission)
🚇 Nieuwmarkt

DE VLIEGENDE SCHOTEL (€€)

Filling soups, salads, noodles and *rijsttafels* are on the menu at 'The Flying Saucer'. Generous portions and good value.

✉ Nieuwe Leliestraat 162–168, Jordaan ☎ 6252041 🕐 Daily 4pm–11pm
🚊 Tram 10

FISH AND VEGETABLES

Although the Dutch eat a lot of meat, Amsterdam with its seagoing associations has a great choice of fish restaurants. Vegetarians, too, have speciality eating places to suit all tastes and budgets, while others, most notably pizzerias and the Asian restaurants around town, offer vegetarian menu-dishes.

International Fare

SURINAMESE CUISINE

Explore the narrow streets of the multiracial district around Albert Cuypstraat, and you will soon realize how easy it is to eat your way around the world in Amsterdam. The many Surinamese restaurants here serve a delicious blend of African, Chinese and Indian cuisine. Specialties include *bojo* (cassava and coconut quiche) and *pitjil* (baked vegetables with peanut sauce). Try them at Marowijne (✉ Albert Cuypstraat 68–70), or Wan Pipel (✉ Albert Cuypstraat 140).

AMSTERDAM (€€)

A beautifully renovated 19th-century water-pumping station is the setting for a cool restaurant, with a menu that's deluge of continental dishes.

✉ Watertorenplein 6, Westerpark ☎ 6822666 🚊 Tram 10

DE BRAKKE GROND (€–€€)

Flemish Cultural Centre's darkly atmospheric restaurant, serving bountiful portions of Belgian food. There is a great choice of Belgian beers to complement your meal.

✉ Nes 43, Centrum ☎ 6260044 🕙 Tue–Sat noon–1am, Sun–Mon noon–7 🚊 Tram 4, 9, 14, 16, 24, 25

CAFÉ PACIFICO (€)

The most authentic Mexican bodega in town. Especially crowded on Tuesday, which is margarita night.

✉ Warmoesstraat 31, Centrum ☎ 6242911 🕙 Centraal Station

CHEZ GEORGES (€€)

Fine Belgian cuisine in a classical, candlelit setting.

✉ Herenstraat 3, Grachtengordel ☎ 6263332 🕙 Closed Sun, Wed 🚊 Tram 1, 2, 5, 6, 13, 17

DYNASTY (€€€)

A sophisticated, sump-tuously decorated garden restaurant with fine Southeast Asian cuisine.

✉ Reguliersdwarsstraat 30, Grachtengordel ☎ 6268400 🕙 Wed–Mon dinner only 🚊 Tram 16, 24, 25

EL RANCHO ARGENTINIAN (€€)

Sizzling steaks and spare ribs in a wood-panelled, jolly-gaucho setting that brings a taste of the South American pampas to Amsterdam.

✉ Spui 3, Centrum ☎ 6256764 🕙 11am–midnight 🚊 Tram 4, 9, 14, 16, 24, 25

DE FLES BISTRO (€€)

Cosy cellar, full of large wooden tables. A real locals' hangout.

✉ Vijzelstraat 137, Grachtengordel ☎ 6249644 🕙 Dinner only 🚊 Tram 16, 24, 25

FROMAGERIE CRIGNON CULINAIR (€)

Rustic restaurant with eight different types of cheese fondue.

✉ Gravenstraat 28, Centrum ☎ 6246428 🕙 Tue–Sat dinner only 🚊 Tram 4, 9, 14, 16, 24, 25

DE KAS (€€–€€€)

Set in a greenhouse from 1926, this trendy, off-the-beaten-track restaurant serves international dishes with a Mediterranean slant.

✉ Kamerlingh Onneslaan 3, Watergraafsmeer ☎ 4624562 🕙 Mon–Fri 12–3, 6.30–10, Sat 6.30–10 🚊 Tram 9

MEMORIES OF INDIA (€€€)

Tandoori, Moghlai and vegetarian cuisine in a refined colonial setting.

✉ Reguliersdwarsstraat 88, Grachtengordel ☎ 6235710 🕙 Dinner only 🚊 Tram 4, 9, 14, 16, 24, 25

PAKISTAN (€€)

A fine Pakistani restaurant. The menu ranges from traditional, village dishes to highly spiced specialities.

✉ Scheldestraat 100, Rivierenbuurt ☎ 6753976 ⏰ Dinner only 🚊 Tram 12, 25

PASTA E BASTA (€€)

Pasta in chic surroundings, with opera classics.

✉ Nieuwe Speigelstraat 8, Grachtengordel ☎ 4222229 ⏰ Dinner only 🚊 Tram 16, 24, 25

ROSE'S CANTINA (€€)

Excellent value Tex-Mex meals in lively, sociable surroundings. Probably Amsterdam's most crowded restaurant.

✉ Reguliersdwarsstraat 38-40, Grachtengordel ☎ 6259797 ⏰ Dinner only 🚊 Tram 4, 9, 14, 16, 24, 25

SEA PALACE (€€)

Advertised as Europe's first floating restaurant, the Sea Palace is modelled on a Chinese pagoda-style palace.

✉ Oosterdokskade 8, Oost & Oosterdok ☎ 6264777 🚈 Centraal Station

SHERPA (€)

Nepalese/Tibetan restaurant with traditional Himalayan ornaments.

✉ Korte Leidsedwarsstraat 58, Grachtengordel ☎ 6239495 ⏰ Dinner only (lunch in summer) 🚊 Tram 1, 2, 5, 6, 7, 10

SHIBLI (€€€)

Sit on a sofa inside a Bedouin tent, dining on an Arabian banquet.

✉ Oudezijds Voorburgwal 236 ☎ 3308082 ⏰ Wed–Sat

dinner only 🚊 Tram 4, 9, 16, 20, 24, 25

TANGO (€€)

Small, candlelit and on the edge of the Red-Light District. Try the huge, juicy steaks.

✉ Warmoesstraat 49, Centrum ☎ 6272467 ⏰ Dinner only 🚊 Tram 4, 9, 14, 16, 24, 25

TEPPANYAKI NIPPON (€€)

One of Holland's most exclusive Japanese grill-restaurants.

✉ Reguliersdwarsstraat 18–20, Grachtengordel ☎ 6208787 ⏰ Dinner only 🚊 Tram 4, 9, 14, 16, 24, 25

TOSCANINI (€€)

The best Italian food in town. Book well ahead.

✉ Lindengracht 75, Jordaan ☎ 6232813 ⏰ Mon–Sat dinner only 🚊 Tram 3

WILHELMINA-DOK (€€)

The decor at this waterside restaurant is vaguely nautical, the continental food fine, and the view of the IJ channel superb.

✉ Nordwall, Amsterdam-Noord ☎ 6233701 ⛴ IJ ferry to Meeuwenlaan

LE ZINC... ET LES DAMES (€€)

Home-style French cuisine in a converted canalside warehouse. The *tarte tatin* is particularly superb.

✉ Prinsengracht 999, Grachtengordel ☎ 6229044 ⏰ Tue–Sat dinner only 🚊 Tram 4

DUTCH SUSHI

Long before Japanese sushi became fashionable fast food in Europe, the Low Countries already had their own version–raw herring–accompanied by chopped onion and pickles. Be sure to try some at one of the herring stalls dotted around town. Kromhout (at the junction of Singel and Raadhuisstraat), and Volendammer Viswinkel (1e van der Helststraat 60) are considered two of the best.

69

Snacks & *Eetcafés*

A BITE TO 'EET'

Try an *eetcafé* for filling homemade fare—soup, sandwiches and omelettes. Remember that kitchens close around 9pm. Browse market stalls for local delicacies. Most bars offer *borrelhapjes* (mouthfuls with a glass)—usually olives, chunks of cheese or *borrelnoten* (nuts with a savoury coating). More substantial *borrelhapjes* are *bitterballen* (bitter balls), fried balls of vegetable paste; and *vlammetjes* (little flames), spicy mini spring rolls. For a really quick snack, the many Febo company's food dispensers about town are cheap: Simply put your money in and your snack comes out hot.

CAFÉ DANTZIG (€)

Sample the giant, crusty baguettes with delicious fillings for lunch on the terrace beside the Amstel river.

✉ Zwanenburgwal 15, Centrum ☎ 6209039 🕔 10am–1am (also Fri, Sat until 2am) 🚇 Waterlooplein

DE EENHOORN (€)

A charming delicatessen-cum-*eetcafé* with wines, cheeses, cold cuts, pâtés.

✉ Warmoesstraat 16, Centrum ☎ 6230878 🕔 Mon–Sat 10–6 🚇 Centraal Station

GARY'S MUFFINS (€)

Fresh filled bagels, muffins and brownies.

✉ Prinsengracht 454, Grachtengordel ☎ 4201452 🕔 Mon–Fri 9–5.30, Sat–Sun 9–6 🚋 Tram 1, 2, 5, 6, 13, 17

LUNCHROOM DIALOGUE (€)

A warehouse cellar, away from the crowds at Anne Frankhuis next door; good for sandwiches and cakes.

✉ Prinsengracht 261a, Grachtengordel ☎ 6239991 🕔 Mon–Sat 9.30–5, Sun 10–5 🚋 Tram 6, 13, 14, 17

MORITA-YA (€)

Traditional Japanese snackbar that's a must for sushi fans.

✉ Zeedijk 18, Centrum ☎ 6380756 🕔 Thu–Tue dinner only 🚇 Centraal Station

PANCAKE BAKERY (€)

The best pancakes in town, and a good place to take the children.

✉ Prinsengracht 191, Grachtengordel ☎ 6251333 🚋 Tram 6, 13, 14, 17

LA PLACE (€)

A self-service 'indoor market' restaurant. Choose your dish at one of the stands, watch it being cooked, then eat at the tables.

✉ Rokin 164, Centrum ☎ 6202364 🕔 10–8 (Thu 10.30–9, Sun–Mon 11–8) 🚋 Tram 4, 9, 14, 16, 24, 25

SMALL TALK (€€)

Near Museumplein, this *eetcafé* is ideal for snacks between gallery visits.

✉ Van Baerlestraat 52, Oud Zuid ☎ 6714864 🕔 Mon–Sat 10–9.30, Sun 10–8.30 🚋 Tram 2, 3, 5, 12

TAPAS CATALÀ (€)

Enjoy a quick bite or a meal of tempting Catalan tapas dishes.

✉ Spuistraat 299, Centrum ☎ 6231141 🕔 Mon, Wed–Fri 4pm–midnight, Sat–Sun 1pm–midnight 🚋 Tram 1, 2, 5

VAN ALTENA (€)

For the finest Dutch raw herring, other seafood snacks, and even a glass of fine wine, visit this sophisticated stand beside the Rijksmuseum.

✉ Stadhouderskade (at Jan Luijkenstraat), Oud Zuid ☎ 6769139 🕔 Tue–Sun 11–7 🚋 Tram 6, 7, 10

VAN DOBBEN (€)

A renowned sandwich shop. Try the meat croquette roll that Van Dobben himself makes from a decades-old recipe.

✉ Korte Reguliersdwarsstraat 5–9, Grachtengordel ☎ 6244200 🕔 Mon–Thu 9.30am–1am, Fri–Sat 9.30am–2am, Sun 11.30am–8pm 🚋 Tram 4, 9, 14

Cafés & Tea Shops

1E KLAS (€)
This café (pronounced 'Eerste Klas') is located on Platfdrm Two in the old first-class waiting rooms at Amsterdam's Centraal Station. Enjoy coffee and cakes in the grand old style of steam travel.
✉ Centraal Station, Stationsplein 15 ☎ 6250131
🕐 9am–11pm 🚊 Centraal Station 🚋 Tram 1, 2, 4, 5, 6, 9, 13, 16, 17, 24, 25

CAFÉ AMÉRICAIN (€)
Artists, writers and bohemians frequent this grand art-deco café.
✉ American Hotel, Leidseplein 26, Grachtengordel
☎ 5563232 🕐 7am–1am
🚋 Tram 1, 2, 5, 6, 7, 10

CAFFÉ ESPRIT (€)
Designer café, all glass and aluminium, run by the clothing chain next door.
✉ Spui 10a, Centrum
☎ 6221967 🕐 Mon–Sat 10–6 (also Thu until 10pm), Sun noon–6 🚋 Tram 1, 2, 4, 5, 9, 14, 16, 24, 25

CAFÉ VERTIGO (€€)
Brown café-style surroundings, where menu-dishes occasionally reflect themes in the Film Museum. Lovely terrace.
✉ Vondelpark 3, Oud Zuid
☎ 6123021 🚋 Tram 1, 3, 12

GELATERIA JORDINO (€)
Bright and breezy place that does great home-made Italian ice cream and waistline-threatening chocolate cake.
✉ Haarlemmerdijk 25, Centrum
☎ 4203225 🕐 10–8
🚌 Bus 18, 22

GREENWOOD'S (€)
Homey little English-style tearoom serving up scones with jam and cream, chocolate cake and lemon-meringue pie.
✉ Singel 103, Grachtengordel
☎ 6237071 🕐 9.30–7
🚋 Tram 1, 2, 5, 6, 13, 17

NIEUWE KAFÉ (€)
The café's crowded terrace on the Dam provides a captive audience for street musicians; ideal for people-watching.
✉ Eggertstraat 8, Centrum
☎ 6272830 🕐 9–6
🚋 Tram 4, 9, 14, 16, 24, 25

POMPADOUR (€)
The finest chocolatier in town doubles as a sumptuous tearoom.
✉ Huidenstraat 12, Grachtengordel ☎ 6239554
🕐 Tue–Fri 9.30–5.45, Sat 9–5.30 🚋 Tram 1, 2, 5

LA RUCHE (€)
Treat yourself to coffee with waffles piled high with strawberries and cream in this café in De Bijenkorf department store (► 74), overlooking the Dam.
✉ 1 Dam, Centrum
☎ 6218080 🕐 Mon 11–6, Tue, Sat 9.30–6, Thu–Fri 9.30–9, Sun noon–6 🚋 Tram 4, 9, 14, 16, 24, 25

WINKEL (€)
A popular café by the Noordermarkt (► 55). Great for people-watching when the markets are on.
✉ Noordermarkt 43, Jordaan
☎ 6230223 🕐 Closed Sat, Mon lunch, all day Sun 🚋 Tram 3, 10

COFFEE SHOPS

In Amsterdam, the expression 'coffee shop' refers to the 'smoking' coffee shops, where mostly young people hang out, high on hash. 'Smoking' coffee shops are usually easily recognizable by their psychedelic decor, thick fog of bitter smoke and mellow clientele. The cake on sale is sure to be drug-laced 'space cake'. Surprisingly, many such shops do a good cup of coffee.

Shopping Areas

SHOPPING TIPS

Although Amsterdam does not compare with Paris or London for European chic, the large number of unusual specialist shops, second-hand shops and colourful markets among its more than 10,000 shops and department stores, make shopping a real pleasure. Interesting souvenirs and gifts to take home are easy to find, whatever your budget.

Most shops are open Tuesday to Saturday from 9am or 10am until 6pm, on Mondays from 1pm until 6pm, on Thursdays until 9pm. Many shops open noon–5pm on Sundays, too. Cash is the usual method of payment, although credit cards are accepted at most department stores and larger shops.

DUTCH GIFTS

Bulbs
Made-to-measure clogs
Bottle of *jenever* (Dutch gin)
Edam or Gouda cheese
Diamonds
Leerdam crystal
Makkum pottery
An old print or map of the city
Delftware—if you want the real thing look for De Porcelyne Fles from Delft itself (► 21).

ART & ANTIQUES

Antique shops are concentrated in the *Spiegelkwartier* near Museumplein, along and by Nieuwe Spiegelstraat and along Rokin. Countless galleries are scattered throughout the city, although many can be found along the main canals. The De Looier Kunst- & Antiekcentrum on Elandsgracht in the Jordaan brings together dozens of art and antiques dealers in an indoor market. Other places to buy art, though not originals, are museum shops that sell high-quality poster reproductions of the famous artworks on their walls, by both Dutch and international artists. Look for the best of these at the Rijksmuseum (small selection until 2008), Van Gogh Museum, Stedelijk Museum and Museum Het Rembrandthuis.

BOOKSHOPS

Most bookshops, including the American Book Center and a branch of British chain Waterstone's in Kalverstraat, are around the university district (off Spui) and in Leidsestraat. You will also find several specialist antique bookshops on Nieuwezijds Voorburgwal, and there is an indoor antiquarian book market at Oudemanhuispoort.

FASHION

The three main shopping thoroughfares—Kalverstraat, Nieuwendijk, and Leidsestraat—are lined with international chain stores and mainstream outlets for clothing and accessories. To the south, you'll find designer stores, including Armani, Azorro and Rodier, along P C Hooftstraat, van Baerlestraat and Beethovenstraat. For more adventurous garb, head for the Jordaan.

OFFBEAT SHOPS

Tiny specialist shops and boutiques selling everything from psychedelic mushrooms to designer soap and kitsch toilet furniture can be found all over the city. Many are in the Jordaan and along the web of sidestreets that connect the ring canals between Leidsegracht and Brouwersgracht.

SECOND-HAND

Explore the second-hand shops of the Jordaan for a bargain, or sift through local street markets, including the city's largest and wackiest flea market at Waterlooplein.

SHOPPING MALLS

There are five main shopping malls: Chic Magna Plaza near the Dam; De Amsterdamse Poort, reached by metro at Amsterdam Zuidoost; Winkelcentrum Boven't IJ, reached by ferry across the IJ; Winkelcentrum Amstelveen in the southern suburbs, reached by tram 5; and Schiphol Plaza at the airport, open from 7am until 10pm daily.

Dutch Souvenirs

AMSTERDAM SMALLEST GALLERY

An original painting of the city bought here will remind you of your stay.
✉ Westermarkt 60
☎ 6223756 🚊 Tram 6, 13, 14, 17

BLUE GOLD FISH

Storehouse of fantastical gifts including jewellery, ornaments, home fixtures and fabrics.
✉ Rozengracht 17
☎ 6233134 🚊 Tram 6, 13, 14, 17

BONEBAKKER

Holland's royal jewellers, with dazzling displays of gold and silverware. Enjoyable even if you can't afford to buy.
✉ Rokin 88–90 ☎ 6232294
🚊 Tram 4, 9, 14, 16, 24, 25

DAM SQUARE SOUVENIRS

This souvenir shop has a wide choice of clogs, furnishings, pottery and T-shirts.
✉ Dam 17 ☎ 6203432
🚊 Tram 4, 9, 14, 16, 24, 25

GALLERIA D'ARTE RINASCIMENTO

For all kinds, and quality, of Delftware, from the most expensive products of DePorcelyne Fles to cheap souvenirs, and for excellent polychrome Makkumware.
✉ Prinsengracht 170
☎ 6227509 🚊 Tram 6, 13, 14, 17

HEINEN HANDPAINTED DELFTWARE

Tiny but delightful for its Delftware plates, tulip vases and Christmas decorations.
✉ Prinsengracht 440
☎ 6278299 🚊 Tram 1, 2, 5, 5, 13, 17

HOLLAND GALLERY DE MUNT

Miniature ceramic canal houses, dolls in traditional costume, ornately decorated wooden boxes and trays. Also antique Delftware; royal and Makkumer pottery; and traditional tiles.
✉ Muntplein 12 ☎ 6232271
🚊 Tram 4, 9, 14, 16, 24, 25

DE KLOMPENBOER

Authentic clog factory offers the city's largest selection of hand-crafted footwear.
✉ Sint-Antoniesbreestraat 51
☎ 6230632 🚊 Tram 1, 2, 5, 6, 13, 17

METZ & CO

Expensive gifts and designer furniture. One of the city's most stylish department stores. It has a café on the top floor.
✉ Keizersgracht 455
☎ 5207020 🚊 Tram 1, 2, 5

STOELTIE DIAMONDS

A tour of the diamond-polishing workshop and a brief history of diamonds, leads inevitably to the sales room.
✉ Wagenstraat 13–17
☎ 6237601 🚊 Tram 4, 9, 14

DE TUIN

The Bloemenmarkt (► 40) is the least expensive place to buy bulbs and this stall has the widest selection.
✉ Bloemenmarkt (opposite Singel 502) ☎ 6254571
🚊 Tram 4, 9, 14, 16, 24, 25

TAX-FREE SHOPPING

If you live outside the European Union, you may claim a tax refund of 13.5 per cent on purchases of €137 or more in one shop in one day. At shops bearing the Tax-Free Shopping logo, ask for a Global Refund Cheque when you pay.

You must export your purchases within 3 months of buying them. At departure to a non-European Union country, go to customs and present your purchases and receipts to have your Global Refund Check validated. You can obtain a cash refund in Schiphol's departure hall, or arrange for a charge-card credit or certified cheque. You should allow around an hour to do this.

If you are travelling by train or car from Holland, you need to go through this procedure at your point of exit from the European Union (if you want to take advantage of the refund scheme). You cannot validate the shopping cheque at Holland's borders with neighbouring countries, because they are EU members.

Food, Drink & Department Stores

SAY CHEESE!

Think Dutch cheese and the distinctive *Edammer* (from Edam) and *Goudse* (from Gouda) spring to mind. They can be young (*jong*) and mild, or more mature (*belegen*) and strong. Mild young cheeses such as *Leerdammer* and *Maaslander* deserve a tasting, too. Others to try are *Friese Nagelkaas*, flavoured with cumin and cloves and *Gras Kaas* (grass cheese), sold in summer, which owes its especially creamy flavour to the freshness of spring's cow pastures.

DE BIERKONING
950 beers and glasses from around the world.
✉ Paleisstraat 125
☎ 6252336 🚊 Tram 1, 2, 5, 6, 13, 14, 17

DE BIJENKORF
Amsterdam's busy main department store, the *Bijenkorf* (Beehive) lives up to its name.
✉ Dam 1 ☎ 6218080
🚊 Tram 4, 9, 14, 16, 24, 25

EICHHOLTZ
Established delicatessen with Dutch, American, and English specialities.
✉ Leidsestraat 48
☎ 6220305 🚊 Tram 1, 2, 5

GEELS EN CO
Holland's oldest coffee-roasting and tea-trading company, full of heady aromas, with a helpful staff and traditional setting.
✉ Warmoesstraat 67
☎ 6240683 🚊 Tram 4, 9, 14, 16, 24, 25

H. P. DE VRENG
Celebrated wine-and-spirits establishment, producing fine liqueurs and *jenevers* since 1852.
✉ Nieuwendijk 75
☎ 6244581 🚊 Tram 1, 2, 5, 6, 13, 17

J. G. BEUNE
Famous for chocolate versions of *Amsterdammertjes* (the posts lining the streets to prevent cars parking on the pavement), and a mouth-watering array of cakes and other bonbons.
✉ Haarlemmerdijk 156
☎ 6248356 🚊 Tram 1, 2, 5, 6, 13, 17

JORDINO
Gorgeous creations in marzipan or chocolate plus home-made ice cream.
✉ Haarlemmerdijk 25a
☎ 4203225 🚊 Tram 1, 2, 5, 6, 13, 17

MAISON DE BONNETERIE
A gracious department store, popular with wealthy ladies.
✉ Rokin 140–2/Kalverstraat 183 ☎ 5313400 🚊 Tram 4, 9, 14, 16, 24, 25

VITALS VITAMIN-ADVICE SHOP
Vitamins and other food supplements, plus a unique service: A computerized test that proposes vitamin supplements based on age and lifestyle.
✉ Nieuwe Nieuwstraat 47
☎ 6257298 🚊 Tram 1, 2, 5, 6, 13, 17

VROOM & DREESMAN
Clothing, jewellery, perfumes, electronics, leather goods, watches, clothing for all the family and household goods. V&D has good quality at reasonable prices.
✉ Kalverstraat 201-203
☎ 6220171 🚊 Tram 4, 9, 14, 16, 20, 24, 25

DE WATERWINKEL
A hundred different mineral waters.
✉ Roelof Hartstraat 10
☎ 6755932 🚊 Tram 3, 5, 12, 24

WOUT ARXHOEK
One of the best cheese shops, with over 250 different varieties.
✉ Damstraat 19 ☎ 6229118
🚊 Tram 4, 9, 14, 16, 20, 24, 25

Antiques & Books

AMERICAN BOOK CENTER
Four floors of English-language books, plus US and British magazines and newspapers.
✉ Kalverstraat 185
☎ 6255537 🚊 Tram 4, 9, 14, 16, 24, 25

AMSTERDAM ANTIQUES GALLERY
Six dealers under one roof, selling silver, pewter, paintings and Dutch tiles, among other items.
✉ Nieuwe Spiegelstraat 34
☎ 6253371 🚊 Tram 6, 7, 10

ATHENAEUM BOEKHANDEL
This bookshop, in a striking art-nouveau building, specializes in social sciences, literature and the classics, and stocks international newspapers.
✉ Spui 14–16 ☎ 6226248
🚊 Tram 1, 2, 5

EDUARD KRAMER
Old Dutch tiles, the earliest dating from the 1500s.
✉ Nieuwe Spiegelstraat 64
☎ 6230832 🚊 Tram 6, 7, 10

EGIDIUS ANTIQUARISCHE BOEKHANDEL
A tiny shop packed with antique books on travel, photography and the arts.
✉ Nieuwezijds Voorburgwal 334
☎ 6243929 🚊 Tram 1, 2, 5

DE KINDER-BOEKWINKEL
Children's books, arranged according to age.
✉ Rozengracht 34
☎ 6224761 🚊 Tram 6, 13, 14, 17

LAMBIEK
The world's oldest comic shop.
✉ Kerkstraat 119
☎ 6267543 🚊 Tram 1, 2, 5

DE LOOIER KUNST- & ANTIEKCENTRUM
A covered antiques market with hundreds of stalls selling everything from quality items to junk.
✉ Elandsgracht 109
☎ 6249038 🚊 Tram 7, 10, 17

PREMSELA & HAMBURGER
Fine antique jewellery and silver in a refined setting.
✉ Rokin 98 ☎ 6249688
🚊 Tram 4, 9, 14, 16, 24, 25

SCHELTEMA, HOLKEMA EN VERMEULEN
The city's biggest bookshop, with a floor of computer software, and audio and video titles.
✉ Koningsplein 20
☎ 5231411 🚊 Tram 1, 2, 5

DE SLEGTE
Amsterdam's largest second-hand bookshop is good for bargains.
✉ Kalverstraat 48–52
☎ 6225933 🚊 Tram 4, 9, 14, 16, 24, 25

WATERSTONE'S
English-language bookshop plus English newspapers and magazines and good guidebooks selection.
✉ Kalverstraat 152
☎ 6383821 🚊 1, 2, 4, 5, 9, 14, 16, 24, 25

GOING, GOING, GONE!
Amsterdam's main auction houses are Sotheby's (✉ De Boelelaan 30 ☎ 5502200) and Christie's (✉ Cornelis Schuytstraat 57 ☎ 5755255). Their Dutch counterpart, Veilinghuis (Auction House) de Nieuwe Zon, is at Elandsgracht (☎ 6230343). All hold presale viewings, interesting even if you have no intention of buying.

Specialist Shops

MAGNA PLAZA

Amsterdam's most luxurious shopping mall, Magna Plaza, is in an imposing neo-Gothic building, which was formerly the city's main post office, in Nieuwezijds Voorburgwal near the Dam. Its four floors are filled with upmarket specialist shops, such as Pinokkio, for educational toys; Bjorn Borg, for sporty underwear; and Speeldozenwereld, for quaint musical boxes. There is a café on the top floor.

ANIMATION ART

Drawings, paintings and figurines of famous cartoon characters from Superman to Tintin and the Smurfs.
✉ Nieuwendijk 91–93
☎ 6222203 ▣ Tram 1, 2, 4, 5, 9, 13, 16, 17, 24, 25

BEADIES

Do-it-yourself jewellery: Choose from a huge range of colourful beads to create your own bracelets or necklaces.
✉ Huidenstraat 6 ☎ 4285161
▣ Tram 1, 2, 5, 6, 13, 17

DE BEESTENWINKEL

A cuddly-toy shop for adults. Ideal for collectors and small gifts.
✉ Staalstraat 11 ☎ 6231805
▣ Tram 4, 9, 14, 16, 24, 25

CONCERTO

Finest all-round selection of new and used records and CDs to suit all tastes. Especially good for jazz, classical music and hits from the 1950s and '60s.
✉ Utrechtsestraat 52–60
☎ 6235228 ▣ Tram 4

CONSCIOUS DREAMS

Anything's possible in Amsterdam. This is just one of several shops that specializes in 'magic mushrooms'.
✉ Kerkstraat 93 ☎ 6266907
▣ Tram 1, 2, 5

CORTINA PAPIER

Stocks all kinds of notebooks, from plain to leather-bound, along with fine paper and writing materials.
✉ Reestraat 22 ☎ 6236676
▣ Tram 6, 13, 14, 17

DE FIETSENMAKER

One of the top bike shops in Amsterdam.
✉ Lauriergracht 50
☎ 6258352 ▣ Tram 6, 13, 14, 17

FIFTIES-SIXTIES

A jumble of period pieces including toasters, records, lamps and other mementos of this hip era.
✉ Reestraat 5 ☎ 6232653
▣ Tram 6, 13, 14, 17

FROZEN FOUNTAIN

Not only is this striking interiors shop a dazzling showcase for up-and-coming Dutch designers, it is a fabulous place for finding unusual gifts, ceramics and jewellery.
✉ Prinsengracht 629 ☎ 622 9375 ▣ Tram 1, 2, 5

DEN HAAN & WAGENMAKERS

A quilt-maker's paradise of traditional fabrics, tools and gadgets.
✉ Nieuwezijds Voorburgwal 97–9 ☎ 6202525 ▣ Tram 1, 2, 5, 6, 13, 17

HEAD SHOP

The shop for marijuana paraphernalia and memorabilia ever since it opened in the 1960s.
✉ Kloveniersburgwal 39
☎ 6249061 ▣ Nieuwmarkt

HEMP WORKS

Designer hemp shop: jeans, jackets, shirts, shampoo and soap all made of hemp. .
✉ Nieuwendijk 13
☎ 4211762 ▣ Tram 1, 2, 5, 6, 13, 17

JACOB HOOIJ

Old-fashioned apothecary,

selling herbs, spices and homeopathic remedies since 1743.

✉ Kloveniersburgwal 12
☎ 6243041 Ⓜ Nieuwmarkt

KITSCH KITCHEN SUPERMERCADO

Ghanaian metal furniture, Indian bead curtains, Mexican tablecloths, Chinese pots and pans—the whole world in one colourful kitchen! An amazing variety of goods on sale including masses of plastic.

✉ Rozengracht 8–12
☎ 4284969 🚊 Tram 6, 13, 14, 17

NIC NIC

Irresistible knick-knacks shop selling 1950s to 1970s collectables and near-antiques, all in good condition.

✉ Gasthuismolensteeg 5
☎ 6228523 🚊 Tram 1, 2, 5

OTTEN & ZOON

Some Dutch people still clomp around in wooden *klompen* (clogs). This shop makes fine wearable ones as well as souvenirs.

✉ Eerste Van der Helsstraat 31
☎ 6629724 🚊 Tram 16, 24, 25

OUTRAS COISAS

Ancient and modern pots and gardening tools, reflecting the Dutch passion for plants.

✉ Herenstraat 31 ☎ 6257281
🚊 Tram 1, 2, 5, 6, 13, 17

PARTY HOUSE

A cornucopia of paper decorations, dressing-up clothes, masks and practical jokes.

✉ Rozengracht 92
☎ 6261054 🚊 Tram 6, 13, 14, 17

P. G. C. HAJENIUS

One of the world's finest tobacco shops, in elegant, art-deco premises; in business for over 250 years.

✉ Rokin 92–96 ☎ 6259985
🚊 Tram 4, 9, 14, 16, 24, 25

POL'S POTTEN

A comucopia of imaginative household fittings, both house-designed and imported, ranging from pottery to furnishings.

✉ KNSM-laan 39 ☎ 3628838
🚊 Tram 10, IJtram

LA SAVONNERIE

A veritable pot-pourri of bathtime products and accessories. You can even have your own personal text inscribed on the delicious handmade soaps.

✉ Prinsengracht 294
☎ 4281139 🚊 Tram 6, 13, 14, 17

SCALE TRAIN HOUSE

Take home a do-it-yourself windmill or canal barge kit as a souvenir, or choose from the vast stock of model railway components.

✉ Bilderdijkstraat 94
☎ 6122670 🚊 Tram 3, 12, 13, 14

DE SPEELMUIS

A splendid collection of handmade wooden toys and doll's house miniatures.

✉ Elandsgracht 58
☎ 6385342 🚊 Tram 6, 7, 10, 17

Fashion

BARGAINS

There are often excellent bargains to be found in Amsterdam, especially during the January and July sales. Keep an eye out for signs saying *Uitverkoop* (closing-down or end-of-season sale), *Solden* (sale) and *Korting* (discounted goods).

ABSOLUTE DANNY
Erotic clothing and accessories with a distinctive design sensibility and a touch of class.
✉ Oudezijds Achterburgwal 78 ☎ 4210915 Ⓜ Nieuwmarkt

ANALIK
Simple, elegant designs are the hallmark of this boutique belonging to Anakujm, Amsterdam's foremost young designer.
✉ Hartenstraat 36 ☎ 4220561 🚊 Tram 1, 2, 5, 6, 13, 14, 17

CORA KEMPERMAN
Elegant and imaginative, fashionable yet Bohemian, individually designed women's fashion.
✉ Leidsestraat 72 ☎ 6251284 🚊 Tram 1, 2, 5

ESPRIT
Young, trendy designs for the seriously fashionable.
✉ Spui 10a ☎ 6263624 🚊 Tram 1, 2, 5

HESTER VAN EEGHEN
Handbags, wallets and other leather accessories in innovative shapes, styles and colours, designed in Holland and made in Italy.
✉ Hartenstraat 37 ☎ 6269212 🚊 Tram 6, 13, 14, 17

MEXX
Top designer boutique where you'll find many leading French and Italian labels.
✉ P C Hooftstraat 118 ☎ 6750171 🚊 Tram 2, 3, 5, 12

OGER
One of the top menswear boutiques.
✉ P C Hooftstraat 81 ☎ 6768695 🚊 Tram 2, 3, 5, 12

OILILY
Children will likely love the brightly coloured and patterned sporty clothes of this Dutch company.
✉ P C Hooftstraat 131–133 ☎ 6723361 🚊 Tram 2, 3, 5, 12

OSCAR
Outrageous footwear, from glittery platforms to psychedelic thigh boots.
✉ Nieuwendijk 208–10 ☎ 6253143 🚊 Tram 4, 9, 14, 16, 24, 25

PALETTE
What's said to be the smallest shop in the Netherlands has a large selection of silk and satin shoes, in 500 colours.
✉ Nieuwezijds Voorburgwal 125 ☎ 6393207 🚊 Tram 4, 9, 14, 16, 24, 25

RETRO
Way-out fashion, including a dazzling array of 1960s and '70s flower-power clothing.
✉ Tweede Constantijn Huygensstraat 57 ☎ 6834180 🚊 Tram 1, 3, 6, 12

SISSY-BOY
Dutch clothing chain with stylish, affordable clothing for men and women.
✉ Leidsestraat 15 ☎ 6238949 🚊 Tram 1, 2, 5

WEBER'S HOLLAND
Fantastical and occasionally straight-out bizarre clothing and accessories, in the historic setting of the Klein Trippenhuis.
✉ Kloveniersburgwal 26 ☎ 6381777 Ⓜ Nieuwmarkt

Theatre, Dance & Cinema

THEATRE & DANCE

BOOM CHICAGO

Very popular comedy theatre with bar and restaurant. Sketches and improvisation, all in English every night, plus late shows in summer.

✉ Leidseplein 12 ☎ 4230101
🚊 Tram 1, 2, 5, 6, 7, 10

FELIX MERITIS

An important avant-garde dance and drama centre, and home to the Felix Meritis experimental theatre company.

✉ Keizersgracht 324
☎ 6231311 🚊 Tram 6, 13, 14, 17

DE KLEINE KOMEDIE

The very best cabaret and stand-up comedy, in one of the city's oldest theatres.

✉ Amstel 56 ☎ 6240534
🚊 Tram 4, 9, 14

KONINKLIJK THEATER CARRÉ

The Royal Theatre hosts long-running international musicals, revues, cabaret, folk dancing and an annual Christmas circus.

✉ Amstel 115–25
☎ 6225225 🚇 Weesperplein

MUZIEKTHEATER

An Amsterdam cultural mainstay and home to the Nederlands Opera and the Nationale Ballet since it opened in 1986, Holland's largest auditorium, seating 1,689, mounts an international repertoire as well as experimental works. There are guided backstage tours on Wednesdays and Saturdays at 3pm (➤ 57).

✉ Waterlooplein 22
☎ 6255455 (recorded information in Dutch; hold for operator) 🚇 Waterlooplein

STADSSCHOUWBURG

Classical and modern plays form the main repertoire of the stylish, 19th-century Municipal Theatre.

✉ Leidseplein 26 ☎ 6242311
🚊 Tram 1, 2, 5, 6, 7, 10

VONDELPARK OPENLUCHTTHEATER

The open-air theatre in the park offers free drama, cabaret, concerts and children's programmes from June to August.

✉ Vondelpark ☎ 6731499
🚊 Tram 1, 2

FILMS

CITY 1–7

A multiscreen cinema, just off Leidseplein.

✉ Kleine Gartmanplantsoen 15
☎ 6234570 🚊 Tram 1, 2, 5, 6, 7, 10

FILM MUSEUM CINEMATHEEK

International programmes, ranging from silent films to more recent releases.

✉ Vondelpark 3 ☎ 5891400
🚊 Tram 1, 3, 12

TUCHINSKI THEATER

Holland's most attractive and prestigious cinema, with six screens. The classic art-deco interior, complete with eight-person boxes and champagne, alone makes it worth visiting, no matter what's showing.

✉ Reguliersbreestraat 26–28
☎ 6262637
🚊 Tram 4, 9, 14, 20

FILM GUIDE

The city's main multiscreen cinema complexes, in the Leidseplein and Rembrandtplein areas, follow Hollywood's lead closely. The latest big US releases and British films that become international hits are sure to show up on Amsterdam's screens after a short delay. Films from other countries occasionally make it to the screen.

Almost all films are shown in their original language, with Dutch subtitles; an important exception is children's films, which are largely sreened in Dutch.

Classical Music & Opera

TICKET TIME

For theatre and concert performances at popular venues you generally need to book ahead. This can be done in person or by telephone to ticket reservation centres. From abroad tickets can be booked directly through the National Reservations Centre ☎ 31 70 3202500. For information and tickets, contact the Amsterdam Uit Buro's Ticketshop (✉ Leidseplein 26 ☎ 0900 0191 www.uitlijn.nl ⏰ Office open daily 10–6, Thu until 9; telephone answered 9–9 daily). Tickets for most performances can also be purchased from the VVV tourist offices and some hotels can book tickets for guests. The daily newspapers and listings magazine *Uitkrant* have programme details.

BEURS VAN BERLAGE

Home to the Netherlands Philharmonic Orchestra and Dutch Chamber Orchestra, this remarkable early modernist building that once housed the stock exchange now makes an impressive concert hall (▶ 56).
✉ Damrak 213 ☎ 6270466
🚊 Tram 4, 9, 16, 24, 25

CONCERTGEBOUW

One of the world's finest concert halls, the magnificent neoclassical Concertgebouw has wonderful acoustics, making it a favourite with musicians worldwide. Since the Royal Concertgebouw Orchestra made its début in 1888, it has come under the baton of Richard Strauss, Mahler, Ravel, Schönberg and Bernard Haitink to name but a few. It continues to be one of the most respected ensembles in the world.
✉ Concertgebouwplein 2–6
☎ 6718345 🚊 Tram 3, 5, 12, 16

ENGELSE KERK

Weekly baroque and choral concerts.
✉ Begijnhof 48 ☎ 6249665
🚊 Tram 1, 2, 4, 5, 9, 14, 16, 24, 25

MUZIEKGEBOUW AAN 'T IJ

A major international venue for contemporary classical music. There are performances of work by John Cage, Xanakis and other modern music pioneers, and around half the concerts are devoted to modern Dutch compositions.
✉ Muziekgebouw aan 't IJ, Piet Heinkade 1 ☎ 7882010
🚊 Tram IJtram

MUZIEKTHEATER

Major operatic works and experimental opera from the Dutch National Opera and other leading international companies (▶ 57 and 79).
✉ Waterlooplein 22
☎ 6255455 🚇 Waterlooplein

NIEUWE KERK

Frequent lunchtime concerts and exceptional organ recitals by visiting organists, in an atmospheric setting (▶ 39).
✉ Dam ☎ 6268168
🚊 Tram 1, 2, 4, 5, 9, 13, 14, 16, 17, 24, 25

OUDE KERK

Chamber music concerts and organ recitals are held in this old church, where Holland's foremost composer, Jan Pieters zoon Sweelinck (1562–1621) was once organist. Pass by at 4pm on Saturdays, and you may hear a carillon concert (▶ 42).
✉ Oudekerksplein 23
☎ 6258284 🚇 Nieuwmarkt

RAI

This convention centre sometimes stages classical music and opera.
✉ Europaplein ☎ 5491212
🚊 Tram 4

TROPENMUSEUM

Traditional music from developing countries is performed at the museum's Soeterijn Theater (▶ 50).
✉ Linnaeusstraat 2
☎ 5688215 🚊 Tram 6, 9, 10, 14

Live Music

AKHNATON
Funky multicultural youth centre with reggae, rap and salsa dance nights. Be prepared for close dancing —this place gets full.
✉ Nieuwezijds Kolk 25
☎ 6243396 🚊 Tram 1, 2, 5, 6, 13, 17

ALTO JAZZ CAFÉ
One of Amsterdam's best jazz and blues venues. Live music nightly, pricey drinks.
✉ Korte Leidsedwarsstraat 115
☎ 6263249 🚊 Tram 1, 2, 5, 6, 7, 10

BAMBOO BAR
Tiny, dark and smoky, this atmospheric bar plays excellent live music nightly—jazz, rhythm and blues and salsa. Popular for its world music too.
✉ Lange Leidsedwarsstraat 64
☎ 6243993 🚊 Tram 1, 2, 5, 6, 7, 10

BIMHUIS
The place for serious followers of avant-garde, improvisational, and experimental jazz, attracting top international players.
✉ Muziekgebouw ann 't IJ, Piet Heinkade 3
☎ 7882150 🚊 Tram IJtram

BOURBON STREET
Nightly blues and jazz. Friendly staff create a good atmosphere.
✉ Leidsekruisstraat 6–8
☎ 6233440 🚊 Tram 6, 7, 10

BRASIL MUSIC BAR
Brazilian bar with live salsa nightly from 10pm.
✉ Lange Leidsedwarsstraat 70
☎ 6261500 🚊 Tram 1, 2, 5, 6, 7, 10

DE HEEREN VAN AEMSTEL
Prior to events such as The Hagues' North Sea Jazz Festival, you can often see some of the world's great jazz performers here.
✉ Thorbeckeplein 5
☎ 6202173 🚊 Tram 4, 9, 14

HOF VAN HOLLAND
Come here for an evening of Dutch folk music and traditional songs.
✉ Rembrandtplein 5
☎ 6234650 🚊 Tram 4, 9, 14

MALOE MELO
This smoky yet convivial Jordaan bar, Amsterdam's 'home of the blues', belts out some fine rhythms.
✉ Lijnbaansgracht 163
☎ 4204592 🚊 Tram 3, 10

O'REILLY'S IRISH PUB
Choice whiskeys and hearty Irish fare accompanied by jolly folk music.
✉ Paleisstraat 103–105
☎ 6249498 🚊 Tram 1, 2, 5

PARADISO
Amsterdam's best venue for live acts—rock, reggae and pop concerts, in a beautiful old converted church that was once the haunt of 1960s hippies.
✉ Weteringschans 6–8
☎ 6264521 🚊 Tram 6, 7, 10

TWEE ZWAANTJES
Traditional Dutch entertainment off the tourist track in a tiny bar full of accordion-playing, folk-singing Jordaaners. Opens from Thursday to Sunday.
✉ Prinsengracht 114
☎ 6423199 🚊 Tram 6, 13, 14, 17

MELKWEG
Located in a wonderful old dairy building (hence the name *Melkweg* or 'Milky Way') on a canal just off Leidseplein, this off-beat multimedia entertainment complex opened in the 1960s and remains a shrine to alternative culture. Live bands play in the old warehouse most evenings, and there is also a constantly changing programme of unconventional theatre, dance, art and film events. (✉ Lijnbaansgracht 234 ☎ 5318181).

NEW MUSIC
A new star in the city's cultural firmament began to shine early in 2005, with the opening of the Muziekgebouw aan 't IJ. The innovative modern concert hall is an ocean of tinted glass standing on the south shore of the IJ channel, just east of Centraal Station. The former Muziekcentrum De IJsbreker experimental music club has moved here, and the Bimhuis jazz club has taken up premises in an annexe. It's a startling indication of how cosmopolitan Amsterdam has become that these two erstwhile smoky and grungy operations should see their futures in a cutting-edge facility amid the large-scale modern architecture of the redeveloped waterfront. (✉ Piet Heinkade 1, ☎ 7882010, www.muziekgebouw.nl)

Brown Cafés & Other Bars

ANCIENT AND MODERN

Brown cafés, so-called because of their chocolate-coloured walls and dark wooden fittings, are reminiscent of the interiors in Dutch Old Master paintings. Here you can meet the locals in a setting that's *gezellig* (cosy). In stark contrast, there are a growing number of brasserie-like grand cafés, and chic, modern bars, with stylish, spacious interiors. Watch also for the tiny ancient *proeflokalen* tasting bars (originally distillers' private sampling rooms), with ageing barrels and gleaming brass taps, serving a host of gins and liqueurs.

BROWN CAFÉS

HANS EN GRIETJE

A small cosy bar beside one of Amsterdam's prettiest canals.
✉ Spiegelgracht 27
☎ 6241324 🚊 Tram 6, 7, 10

HOPPE

One of Amsterdam's most established, most popular brown cafés, with beer in one bar and gin from the barrel in another.
✉ Spui 18–20 ☎ 4204420
🚊 Tram 1, 2, 5

DE KARPERSHOEK

A sawdust-strewn bar dating from 1629 that once was frequented by sailors.
✉ Martelaarsgracht 2
☎ 6247886 🚇 Centraal Station

HET MOLENPAD

An old-fashioned brown café. The canalside terrace catches the early evening sun.
✉ Prinsengracht 653
☎ 6259680 🚊 Tram 1, 2, 5

PAPENEILAND

Amsterdam's oldest bar has retained its old-world charm with panelled walls, Makkum tiles, candles, benches and a wood-burning stove.
✉ Prinsengracht 2
☎ 6241989 🚊 Tram 1, 2, 5, 6, 13, 17

DE PRINS

Very much a locals' bar, despite its proximity to the Anne Frankhuis, with a cosy pub atmosphere and seasonal menu.
✉ Prinsengracht 124
☎ 6249382 🚊 Tram 6, 13, 14, 17

VAN PUFFELEN

An intimate sawdust-strewn brown bar with a smart restaurant in the back. You can sit on a barge moored outside, on the Prinsengracht, in summer.
✉ Prinsengracht 375–377
☎ 6246270 🚊 Tram 6, 13, 14, 17

REIJNDERS

Brown cafés are typically on tranquil streets; Reijnders is on brash, neon-lit Leidseplein yet has retained much of its traditional style and look.
✉ Leidseplein 6 ☎ 6234419
🚊 Tram 1, 2, 5, 6, 7, 10

GRAND CAFÉS & STYLISH BARS

DE ENGELBEWAARDER

Jazz on Sunday from 4pm livens up a usually tranquil, arty hangout just off the Red-Light District.
✉ Kloveniersburgwal 59
☎ 6253772 🚇 Nieuwmarkt

DE JAREN

A spacious, ultramodern café, known for its trendy clientele. Sunny terraces overlooking the Amstel.
✉ Nieuwe Doelenstraat 20–22
☎ 6255771
🚊 Tram 4, 9, 14, 16, 24, 25

HET LAND VAN WALEM

One of Amsterdam's first modern bars, still tolerably trendy after all these years.
✉ Keizersgracht 449
☎ 6253544 🚊 Tram 1, 2, 5

LUXEMBOURG

Watch the world go by over canapés or colossal club sandwiches on the terrace of this elegant, high-ceilinged bar.

✉ Spui 24 ☎ 6206264
🚊 Tram 1, 2, 5

L'OPERA

Fashionable with the city's chic set, though it's not quite as good as it looks.
✉ Rembrandtplein 27–31
☎ 6275232
🚊 Tram 4, 9, 14

ROYAL CAFÉ DE KROON

Affects a cool, hard-edged modernity as if to belie a location on the rambunctious Rembrandtplein. A great enclosed falcony is its saving grace.
✉ Rembrandtplein 17
☎ 6252011 🚊 Tram 4, 9, 14

SCHILLER

An evocative art-deco bar enhanced with live piano music. Sophisticated for Rembrandtplein.
✉ Rembrandtplein 26
☎ 6249846 🚊 Tram 4, 9, 14

PROEFLOKALEN (TASTING BARS)

CAFÉ HOOGHOUDT

Brown bar-cum-*proeflokaal* in an old warehouse lined with traditional stoneware *jenever* barrels. Tasty Dutch appetizers go with a big selection of liqueurs.
✉ Reguliersgracht 11
☎ 4204041 🕐 4pm–1am
🚊 Tram 4, 9, 14, 16, 24, 25

DE DRIE FLESCHJES

Amsterdammers have been tasting gins at The Three Little Bottles since 1650.
✉ Gravenstraat 18
☎ 6248443 🚊 Tram 1, 2, 4, 5, 6, 9, 13, 14, 16, 17, 24, 25

DE OOIEVAAR

A homey atmosphere pervades The Stork, one of Holland's smallest *proeflokalen*.
✉ Sint-Olofspoort 1
☎ 4208004 🚊 Centraal Station

WYNAND FOCKINK

Hidden down a side alley off the Dam, this charming 1679 *proeflokaal* serves 100 or so gins and liquers, some made at the next-door Janssens distillery (open to visits Mon–Sat 2–6 ☎ 6225334). If the weather is warm, seek out the charming courtyard garden but note, mobile phones are banned.
✉ Pijlsteeg 31 ☎ 6392695
🚊 Tram 4, 9, 14, 16, 24, 25

SPECIALIST BARS

DE BEIAARD

A beer drinker's paradise—over 80 beers from around the world.
✉ Spui 30 ☎ 6225110
🚊 Tram 1, 2, 5

BULLDOG PALACE

Flagship of the Bulldog chain of bars and smoking coffee shops—a plush, loud bar, brashly decked out in stars and stripes. Downstairs is a 'smoking coffeeshop' (▶ panel 71).
✉ Leidseplein 13–17
☎ 6271908 🚊 Tram 1, 2, 5, 6, 7, 10

CAFÉ APRIL

Popular, easy-going gay bar that attracts a mixed crowd of mostly male locals and tourists.
✉ Reguliersdwarsstraat 37
☎ 6259572 🚊 Tram 1, 2, 5

BAR TALK

Most of the 1,402 bars and cafés in Amsterdam are open from around 10am until the early hours and many serve meals. *Proeflokalen* open from around 4pm until 8pm, and some serve snacks, such as nuts, cheese, meatballs and sausage. Beer is the most popular alcoholic drink. It is always served with a head, and often with a *jenever* chaser called a *kopstoot* (a blow to the head). If you want only a small beer, ask for a *colatje* or *kleintjepils*. Dutch for cheers is *Proost!* Belgian beers are increasingly popular in Holland, and are considered more of a craft product.

'DUTCH COURAGE'

Dutch gin (*jenever*), made from molasses and flavoured with juniper berries, comes in a variety of ages: *jong* (young), *oud* (old) and *zeer oud* (the oldest and the mellowest), and in colour ranging from clear to brownish. Other flavours may be added; try *bessenjenever* (blackcurrant), or *bitterkoekjes likeur* (macaroon). *Jenever* is drunk straight or as a beer chaser, not with a mixer.

Nightclubs

GAY AMSTERDAM

Clubbing is at the heart of Amsterdam's gay scene. The best-known venue is iT, a glitzy disco with throbbing techno. Gay bars and clubs abound in nearby Reguliersdwarsstraat and Halvemaansteeg. To find out exactly what's on and where it's happening, call the Gay and Lesbian Switchboard (☎ 6236565) or read the bilingual (Dutch–English) magazines *Gay News* and *Gay & Night*.

NIGHT AT THE TABLES

Try all the usual games, plus Sic Bo (a Chinese dice game) at Holland Casino Amsterdam, one of Europe's largest. There is a small entrance fee and you must be over 18 and present your passport, but there is no strict dress code.
✉ Max Euweplein 62
☎ 5211111 🚊 Tram 1, 2, 5, 6, 7, 10

BACKDOOR

Leading 'non-house' club for R & B, disco, soul, funk and weekly retro theme nights.
✉ Amstelstraat 32
☎ 6202333 🕐 Daily 11pm–5am 🚊 Tram 4, 9, 14

BOSTON CLUB

Attracts a 30s–40s crowd looking for a quieter dancing experience.
✉ Renaissance Hotel, Kattengat 1 ☎ 6245561 🚊 Tram 1, 2, 5, 6, 13, 17

DANSEN BIJ JANSEN

Student disco playing the latest chart toppers. You need student ID or be with a student, to get in.
✉ Handboogstraat 11
☎ 6201779 🕐 Daily 11pm–4am 🚊 Tram 1, 2, 5,

ESCAPE

Amsterdam's largest disco, which can hold 2,000 dancers, has a dazzling light show and superb sound system.
✉ Rembrandtplein 11
☎ 6223542 🕐 10pm–4am (Fri–Sat until 5am) 🚊 Tram 4, 9, 14

iT

The wildest disco in town, with outrageously dressed clientele and fierce house music. Saturday night is exclusively gay.
✉ Amstelstraat 24
☎ 6250111 🕐 Thu, 11pm–4am (Fri–Sat until 5am) 🚊 Tram 4, 9, 14

JANTJES VERJAARDAG

Cool cocktails and hot dancing—to the latest salsa and *merengue* beats.
✉ Amstelstraat 9 ☎ 6251973
🕐 Fri–Sat 11.30pm–5am, Sun until 4am 🚊 Tram 4, 9, 14

KORSAKOFF

Thrash metal and industrial sounds for the leather, chains and piercing crowd—despite which the atmosphere is fun and friendly.
✉ Lijnbaansgracht 161
☎ 6257854 🕐 Daily from 11pm 🚊 Tram 10, 13, 14, 17

MAZZO

A young image-conscious crowd prop up the bar of this small but chic disco in the Jordaan, while guest DJs and live bands play the latest sounds.
✉ Rozengracht 114
☎ 6267500 🕐 11pm–4am (Fri–Sat until 5am) 🚊 Tram 6, 13, 14, 17

MINISTRY

A café-cum-nightclub with all kinds of disco music.
✉ Reguliersdwarsstraat 12
☎ 6233981 🕐 Thu–Mon 10pm–5am 🚊 Tram 1, 2, 4, 5, 9, 14, 16, 24, 25

ODEON

A converted canal house with house music on the first floor, 1960s–'80s classic disco upstairs and jazz in the basement.
✉ Singel 460 ☎ 6249711
🕐 10pm–4am (Fri–Sat until 5am) 🚊 Tram 1, 2, 5

SINNERS IN HEAVEN

Dress smart for this stylish club, with three floors each with different music. Free before midnight.
✉ Wagenstraat 3–7
☎ 6201375 🕐 Thu–Sat from 11pm 🚊 Tram 4, 9, 14

Sport

FISHING

Obtain a permit from the Dutch Fishing Federation to fish in the Amsterdamse Bos (▶ 60).

✉ Nicolaas Witsenstraat 10
☎ 6264988 🚊 Tram 6, 7, 10

FITNESS
JANSEN AEROBIC FITNESSCENTRUM

Fitness centre with gyms, sauna, solarium and daily aerobics classes.

✉ Rokin 109–111
☎ 6269366 🚊 Tram 4, 9, 14, 16, 24, 25

GOLF
GOLFBAAN WATERLAND

Modern 18-hole course north of the city.

✉ Buikslotermeerdijk 141
☎ 6361010

HORSE RIDING
HOLLANDSCHE MANEGE

Amsterdam's most central riding school, dating from 1882, provides riding in the Amsterdamse Bos.

✉ Vondelstraat 140
☎ 6180942 🚊 Tram 1, 6

JOGGING

There are marked trails for joggers through the Vondelpark and Amsterdamse Bos. The Amsterdam Marathon is in May, and the Grachtenloop canal race in June when up to 5,000 run either 5, 10, or 20km (12.5 miles) along the banks of Prinsengracht and on Vijzelgracht.

ICE SKATING

The canals often freeze in winter, turning the city into a big ice rink. Skates can be bought at most sports equipment stores.

JAAP EDENBAAN

A large outdoor ice rink, open October to March.

✉ Radioweg 64 ☎ 6949652
🚊 Tram 9

SWIMMING

The seaside is only 30 minutes away by train, with miles of clean, sandy beaches. Zandvoort is the closest resort; Bergen aan Zee and Noordwijk are also popular.

FLEVOPARKBAD

The best outdoor pool in the city, open from mid-May until late-September.

✉ Insulindeweg 1002
☎ 6925030 🚊 Tram 14

DE MIRANDABAD

Subtropical swimming pool complex with indoor and outdoor pools, beach, wave machines and a restaurant.

✉ De Mirandalaan 9
☎ 5464444 🚊 Tram 25

ZUIDERBAD

This historic indoor pool (built 1912) is conveniently situated a short stroll from the Rijksmuseum and is the perfect place for children to enjoy letting off steam after all that sightseeing.

✉ Hobbemastraat 26
☎ 6710287 🚊 Tram 2, 5

GO-KARTING
KAARTBAAN AMSTERDAM

Great fun for children large and small.

✉ Theemsweg 1, Sloterdijk
☎ 6111642 🚉 Sloterdijk

SPECTATOR SPORTS

Football (soccer) is Holland's number one spectator sport and the number one team is Ajax Amsterdam. Watch them play at their magnificent stadium, the Amsterdam ArenA, (✉ Arena Boulevard, Amsterdam Zuidoost ☎ 3111444). Other popular events include international field hockey at Wagenaar Stadium (✉ Nieuwe Kalfjeslaan ☎ 6401141) and equestrian show-jumping at RAI (✉ Europaplein ☎ 5491212) every November. Look out for a Dutch hybrid of volleyball and netball called *korfball*, and *carambole*— billiards on a table without pockets.

IN-LINE SKATING

Friday night is skating night, when hundreds turn out for a mass skate from Vondelpark when the weather is fine enough. Check out www.fridaynightskate.nl for details. Skates can be hired from Rent A Skate (✉ Vondelpark, at the café by the Amstelveenseweg entrance ☎ mobile 6645091).

Luxury Hotels

PRICES

Expect to pay over €200 a night for a double room in a luxury hotel.

HOTEL TIPS

Two-fifths of Amsterdam's 30,000 hotel beds are in 4- and 5-star properties, making problems for people looking for mid-range and budget accommodation. At peak times, such as during the spring tulip season and summer, empty rooms in lower-cost hotels are about as rare as black tulips. Book ahead for these times. Special offers may be available at other times. Many hotels lower their rates in winter, when the city is quieter and truer to itself than in the mad whirl of summer.

Watch out for hidden pitfalls, such as Golden Age canal houses with four floors, steep and narrow stairways and no lift; and tranquil-looking mansions with a late-night café's pavement terrace next door.

The VVV operates a hotel reservation centre from Mon–Fri 9–5 ☎ (31) 77 700 0088 from outside the Netherlands, 2018800 from within.

AMSTEL INTER-CONTINENTAL

Holland's most luxurious and expensive hotel. 79 rooms.
✉ Prof Tulpplein 1, Amstel ☎ 6226060; www.interconti.com 🚇 Weesperplein 🚋 Tram 6, 7, 10

BILDERBERG GARDEN

In a pleasant leafy suburb, a short tram ride from the heart of the city. 98 rooms.
✉ Dijsselhofplantsoen 7, Oud Zuid ☎ 5705600; www.gardenhotel.nl 🚋 Tram 16

BLAKES AMSTERDAM

A stunning 17th-century conversion designed by Anouska Hempel, based on Dutch and Indonesian themes. 26 rooms.
✉ Keizersgracht 384, Grachtengordel ☎ 5302010; www.blakesamsterdam.com 🚋 Tram 1, 2, 5

CROWNE PLAZA AMSTERDAM–AMERICAN

A resplendent art-nouveau Amsterdam classic sited on the Leidseplein. 188 rooms.
✉ Leidsekade 97, Grachtengordel ☎ 5563000; www.amsterdam-american.crowneplaza.com 🚋 Tram 1, 2, 5, 6, 7, 10

DE L'EUROPE

Prestigious, combining turn-of-the-century architecture with the most modern amenities, in a waterfront setting. 100 rooms.
✉ Nieuwe Doelenstraat 2–8, Centrum ☎ 5311777; www.leurope.nl 🚋 Tram 4, 6, 9, 14, 16, 24, 25

GRAND SOFITEL DEMEURE AMSTERDAM

From 16th-century royal inn to City Hall; now a luxury hotel with a strong sense of history. 182 rooms.
✉ Oudezijds Voorburgwal 197, Centrum ☎ 5553111; www.thegrand.nl 🚇 Nieuwmarkt

HILTON

Modern efficiency on a boulevard to the south. The honeymoon suite was the scene of John Lennon and Yoko Ono's 1969 love-in for world peace. 271 rooms.
✉ Apollolaan 138, Oud Zuid ☎ 7106000; www.amsterdam.hilton.com 🚋 Tram 16

NH BARBIZON PALACE

Modern luxury deftly concealed within a row of 17th-century mansions. 274 rooms.
✉ Prins Hendrikkade 59–72, Centrum ☎ 5564564; www.nh-hotels.com 🚇 Centraal Station

NH GRAND HOTEL KRASNAPOLSKY

Built in the 1880s, the 'Kras' has belle-époque grace in its public spaces and modern facilities in its rooms. 469 rooms.
✉ Dam 9, Centrum ☎ 5549111; www.nh-hotels.com 🚋 Tram 1, 2, 4, 5, 9, 13, 14, 16, 17, 24, 25

PULITZER

Twenty-four 17th-century houses have been converted into this luxurious canalside hotel. 226 rooms.
✉ Prinsengracht 315–331, Grachtengordel ☎ 5235235; www.pulitzer.nl 🚋 Tram 6, 13, 14, 17

Mid-Range Hotels

AMBASSADE
Amsterdam's smartest B&B, in a series of gabled canal houses. 59 rooms.
✉ Herengracht 341, Grachtengordel ☎ 5550222; www.ambassde-hotel.nl 🚊 Tram 1, 2, 5

AMSTERDAM
Fully modernized behind its 18th-century façade, on one of the city's busiest tourist streets. 80 rooms.
✉ Damrak 93–94, Centrum ☎ 5550666; www.amsterdamhotel.nl 🚊 Tram 4, 9, 14, 16, 24, 25

AMSTERDAM HOUSE
Quietly situated small hotel beside the Amstel. Most rooms have a view of the river. 16 rooms.
✉ 's-Gravelandseveer 7, Centrum ☎ 6262579; www.amsterdamhouse.com 🚊 Tram 4, 9, 14, 16, 24, 25

BILDERBERG HOTEL JAN LUYKEN
A well-run, elegant townhouse in a quiet back street near Vondelpark and Museumplein. 65 rooms.
✉ Jan Luijkenstraat 58, Oud Zuid ☎ 5730730; www.janluyken.nl 🚊 Tram 2, 3, 5, 12

CANAL HOUSE
Antique furnishings and a pretty garden make this small, family-run hotel a gem. 26 rooms.
✉ Keizersgracht 148, Grachtengordel ☎ 6225182; www.canalhousehotel.com 🚊 Tram 6, 13, 14, 17

ESTHERÉA
A well-considered blend of wood-panelled canalside character with efficient service and modern facilities. 70 rooms.
✉ Singel 303–309, Grachtengordel ☎ 6245146; www.estherea.nl 🚊 Tram 1, 2, 5

ITC
A quiet gay-orientated, hotel, with a garden, on one of the city's most beautiful canals. 34 rooms.
✉ Prinsengracht 1051, Grachtengordel ☎ 6230230; www.itc-hotel.com 🚊 Tram 4

LLOYDS HOTEL
In a refurbished monument of Amsterdam School architecture from 1921, this innovative hotel opened in 2004 in the harbour redevelopment zone. 120 rooms.
✉ Oostelijke Handelskade 34, Oostelijke Eilanden ☎ 5613636; www.lloydhotel.com 🚊 Tram IJtram

MAAS
A charming, family-run, waterfront hotel near museums, shops and nightlife. 28 rooms.
✉ Leidsekade 91, Grachtengordel ☎ 6233868; www.hotelmaas.nl 🚊 Tram 1, 2, 5, 6, 7, 10

NH DOELEN
Amsterdam's oldest hotel, where Rembrandt painted *The Night Watch;* 85 small well-equipped rooms.
✉ Nieuwe Doelenstraat 24, Centrum ☎ 5540600; www.nh-hotels.com 🚊 Tram 4, 9, 14, 16, 24, 25

SEVEN BRIDGES
Small and exquisite; the owners treat their guests like friends. 11 rooms.
✉ Reguliersgracht 31, Grachtengordel ☎ 6231329 🚊 Tram 4

PRICES
Expect to pay from €100 a night to €200 for a double room in a mid-range hotel.

BED AND BREAKFAST, APARTMENTS AND BOATS
If you want to rent an apartment in Amsterdam, contact Amsterdam House (☎ 6262577; www.amsterdamhouse.com); you can take your pick of luxury apartments in converted canal houses, or even a houseboat. Bed and Breakfast Holland (✉ Theophile de Bockstraat 3 ☎ 6157527; www.bedandbreakfast.com) will set you up with a room in a private house.

DISABILITY-FRIENDLY
The NH City Centre Hotel, with its striking Amsterdam School-style architecture has particularly good facilities for visitors with disabilities.
✉ Spuistraat 288–292, Centrum ☎ 4204545 🚊 Tram 1, 2, 5

Budget Accommodation

PRICES

Expect to pay up to €100 a night for a double room in a budget hotel. Hostels and campsites are considerably cheaper.

CAMPING

There are several campsites in and around Amsterdam. The best-equipped one is a long way out, in the Amsterdamse Bos (✉ Kleine Noorddijk 1, ☎ 6416868). Vliegenbos is just a ten-minute bus ride from the station, close to the IJ waterway (✉ Meeuwenlaan 138, ☎ 6368855). Contact the VVV for full details.

ACACIA

An inexpensive, cheerful, family-run hotel with studio rentals and a pair of houseboats. 14 rooms.
✉ Lindengracht 251, Jordaan
☎ 6221460; www.hotelacacia.nl
🚊 Tram 3

AGORA

Comfortable, 18th-century canal house furnished with antiques and filled with flowers. 16 rooms.
✉ Singel 462, Grachtengordel
☎ 6272200; www.hotelagora.nl
🚊 Tram 4, 9, 14, 16, 24, 25

AMSTEL BOTEL

One of Amsterdam's few floating hotels, with magnificent views over the old docks. 175 rooms.
✉ Oosterdokskade 2–4, Oosterdok ☎ 6264247;
www.amstelbotel.com
🚉 Centraal Station

ARENA

In a handsomely converted 19th-century orphanage, this stylish hotel has a café and restaurant and puts on dance nights, concerts, exhibitions and other events. 121 rooms.
✉ 's-Gravesandestraat 51, Oost and Oosterdok ☎ 6947444;
www.hotelarena.nl 🚊 Tram 7, 10

DE FILOSOOF

All 25 rooms are named after great philosophers and decorated accordingly.
✉ Anna van den Vondelstraat 6, Oud West ☎ 6833013;
www.hotelfilosoof.nl 🚊 Tram 1, 6

NOVA

A clean, simple, central hotel with friendly young staff. 59 rooms.
✉ Nieuwezijds Voorburgwal 276, Centrum ☎ 6230066;
www.novahotel.nl 🚊 Tram 1, 2, 5

OWL

In a quiet street near Vondelpark this family-owned hotel has 34 bright, rooms and a garden.
✉ Roemer Visscherstraat 1, Oud Zuid ☎ 6189484; www.owl-hotel.nl 🚊 Tram 2, 3, 5, 12

PRINSENHOF

Quaint, comfortable and clean; one of the city's best budget options. 11 rooms.
✉ Prinsengracht 810, Grachtengordel ☎ 6231772;
www.hotelprinsenhof.nl
🚊 Tram 4

SINT-NICOLAAS

Rambling former factory and comfortable, if sparse, facilities. 24 rooms.
✉ Spuistraat 1a, Centrum
☎ 6261384;
www.hotelnicolaas.nl 🚊 Tram 1, 2, 5, 6, 13, 17

STAYOKAY AMSTERDAM VONDELPARK

A wide range of modern options, from dormitories to family rooms. 475 rooms.
✉ Zandpad 5, Vondelpark, Oud Zuid ☎ 5898996;
www.stayokay.nl 🚊 Tram 1, 2, 5, 6, 7, 10

VAN OSTADE BICYCLE HOTEL

Small hotel that rents bikes to discover hidden Amsterdam. 16 rooms.
✉ Van Ostadestraat 123, De Pijp
☎ 6793452;
www.bicyclehotel.com
🚊 Tram 3, 12, 25

AMSTERDAM
travel facts

ESSENTIAL FACTS

Electricity
- 220 volts; round two-pin sockets.

Etiquette
- Shake hands on introduction. Once you know people better, you might exchange three pecks on alternate cheeks instead.
- Remember to say *hallo* and *dag* (goodbye) when shopping.
- Dress is generally informal, even for the opera, ballet and theatres.
- Although service charges are included in bills (checks), tipping is customary. Leave a small tip or round up the bill.

Lavatories
- There are few public lavatories. Use the facilities in museums and department stores. There is often a small charge (€0.30–0.50).

Money matters
- Banks may offer a better exchange rate than hotels or independent bureaux de change. GWK (Grenswisselkantoor) offer 24-hour money-changing services at Schiphol Airport and extended hours at Centraal Station.

National holidays
- 1 January; Good Friday, Easter Sunday and Monday; 30 April; Ascension Day; Pentecost and Pentecost Monday; 25 and 26 December.
- 4 and 5 May—Remembrance Day (*Herdenkingsdag*) and Liberation Day (*Bevrijdingsdag*)—are World War II Commemoration Days but not public holidays.

Opening hours
- Banks: Mon–Fri 9 until 4 or 5. Some stay open Thu until 7.
- Shops: Tue–Sat 9 or 10 until 6, Mon 1 to 6. Some open Thu until 9 and Sun noon until 5. Some close early Sat, at 4 or 5.
- State-run museums and galleries: most open Tue–Sat 10 to 5, Sun and national holidays 1 to 5. Many close on Mon.

Places of worship
- Roman Catholic: Parish of the Blessed Trinity, Heilige Familie-kerk ✉ Zouiersweg 180 ☎ 4652711
- English Reformed Church: ✉ Begijnhof 48 ☎ 6249665
- Jewish: Jewish and Liberal Community Amsterdam: ✉ Jacob Soetendorpstraat 8 ☎ 6423562
- Muslim: THAIBA Islamic Cultural Centre: ✉ Kraaiennest 125 ☎ 6982526

Student travellers
- For discounts at some museums, galleries, theatres, restaurants and hotels, students under 26 can obtain an International Young Person's Pass (CJP—Cultureel Jongeren Pass), cost €10, from: AUB ✉ Leidseplein 26 ☎ 0900/0191; and NBBS ✉ Rokin 66 ☎ 6240989

Tourist offices (VVV)
- The three Vereniging voor Vreemdelingenverkeer (VVV) offices and the Holland Tourism International (HTi) desk at Schiphol Airport all have multilingual staff, city maps and brochures. They will also make hotel, excursion, theatre and concert bookings for a small fee. They are:
  Centraal Station VVV
  ✉ Centraal Station, Platform 2)
  Stationsplein VVV
  ✉ Stationsplein 10
  Leidseplein VVV
  ✉ Leidseplein 1

Holland Tourism International

✉ Schiphol Airport

- For enquiries ☎ 0900/4004040;
www.visitamsterdam.nl

GETTING AROUND

Buying and using tickets

- If you intend to use public transport frequently, buy a ticket of 15 or 45 strips (*strippenkaart*), available at GVB and Dutch Railways ticket counters, some newsagents and the VVV. For each ride, a strip must be used for each zone you want to pass through, plus one for the ride: For example, from Centraal Station to Leidseplein is one zone, so you need to count down two strips of your *strippenkaart*, and stamp the second one. Zones are shown on maps at tram, bus and Metro stops.
- On buses: Tell the driver the number of zones you want and your ticket will be stamped.
- On the Metro: Before boarding, fold back the appropriate number of strips and punch your ticket in the yellow ticket machines before entering the platform.
- On trams: Most trams have a conductor at the back who sells and stamps tickets. On other trams either ask the driver to stamp your ticket or do it yourself in a yellow punch-machine.
- For a single trip, purchase a single (1- or 2-zones) ticket, from the driver or conductor of the bus or tram, or from a machine at the Metro entrance. Buy day and other tickets, 2-, 3-, 8-, 15- and 45-strip cards from Metro and train station ticket counters, VVV offices, newsagents and bus/tram drivers/conductors (not all kinds of tickets are available from each

of these sources).

- All city-zones single tickets and strips are valid for one hour after the time stamped on them, and include transfers.
- Don't travel without a valid ticket: You could be fined €30 on the spot.
- For further information and maps, contact GVB Tickets & Info ✉ Stationsplein ☎ 0900/9292

Getting around by bicycle

- The best way to see Amsterdam is by bicycle and the city is geared up to riders on two wheels. To hire one costs from €4.50 a day, €17 a week.
Damstraat Rent-a-Bike ✉ Damstraat 20–22 ☎ 6255029; www.bikes.nl
BikeCity ✉ Bloemgracht 68–70 ☎ 6263721 🕐 Mon–Sat 9–6

MEDIA & COMMUNICATIONS

Mail

- Purchase stamps (*postzegels*) at post offices, tobacconists and souvenir shops.
- Post boxes are bright red and clearly marked 'TPG POST'.

Newspapers and magazines

- The main Dutch newspapers are *De Telegraaf* (right wing), *De Volkskrant* (left wing) and *NRC Handelsblad*.
- The main Amsterdam newspapers (sold nationwide) are *Het Parool* and *Nieuws van de Dag*.
- Listings magazines: *Amsterdam Day by Day* and *Uitkrant*.
- *The Times*, the *Independent* and the *Guardian* are widely available.

Post Offices

- Most post offices open weekdays 8.30 or 9 until 5.

- Main Post Office:
  ✉ HoofdpostkantoorTPG, Singel 250–256
  ☎ 3300555 ⏰ Mon–Fri 9–6 (Thu 9–8),
  Sat 10–1.30
- Postal Information: ☎ 0800/0417

Telephones

- Most public telephones take
  phonecards available from telephone centres, post offices,
  railway stations and newsagents.
- Phone calls within Europe cost
  about €0.35 per minute.
- National directory enquiries:
  ☎ 0900/8008
- International directory enquiries:
  ☎ 0900/0418
- Numbers starting 0900 are pre-
  mium rate calls; 0800 are free;
  0600 are mobile phone numbers.
- Local and international operator:
  ☎ 0800/0410
- To phone abroad, dial 00 then the
  country code (UK 44, US and
  Canada 1, Australia 61, New
  Zealand 64, Ireland 353, South
  Africa 27), then the number.
- Most hotels have International
  Direct Dialling, but it is expensive.
- The code for Amsterdam is 020.
  To phone from outside Holland
  drop the first 0.

EMERGENCIES

Emergency phone numbers

- Police: ☎ 112
- Ambulance: ☎ 112
- Fire Service: ☎ 112
- Tourist Medical Service: ☎ 5923355
- Automobile Emergency (ANWB):
  ☎ 0800/000888
- Lost credit cards: American
  Express ☎ 5048666, Diners Club
  ☎ 0800/0334, Master/Eurocard
  ☎ 030/2835555, Visa ☎ 6600611
- Sexual Advice ☎ 0800/0224176
- Crisis Helpline ☎ 6757575

Embassies and consulates

- American Consulate: ✉ Museumplein
  19 ☎ 6645661
- British Consulate: ✉ Koningslaan 44
  ☎ 6764343
- Canadian Embassy: ✉ Sophialaan 7,
  The Hague ☎ 070/3111600
- Australian Embassy: ✉ Carnegielaan
  4a, The Hague ☎ 070/3108200
- New Zealand Embassy:
  ✉ Carnegielaan 10, The Hague ☎ 070/3469324
- Irish Embassy: ✉ Dr Kuyperstraat 9, The
  Hague ☎ 070/3630993
- South African Embassy:
  ✉ Wassenaarseweg 40, The Hague
  ☎ 070/3924501

Lost property

- For insurance purposes, report
  lost or stolen property to the
  police as soon as possible.
- Main lost property offices:
  Centraal Station ✉ Stationsplein 15
  ☎ 5578544 ⏰ Daily 7am–11pm
  Police Lost Property
  ✉ Stephensonstraat 18 ☎ 5593005 ⏰ Mon–Fri
  noon–3.30
- For property lost on public
  transport, GVB ✉ Prins Hendrikkade
  108–14 ☎ 4605858 ⏰ Mon–Fri 9–4

Medicines

- For non-prescription drugs, and so
  on, go to a *drogist*. For prescription
  medicines, go to an *apotheek*, most
  open Mon–Fri 8.30–5.30.
- Details of pharmacies open outside normal hours are in the daily
  newspaper *Het Parool* and all
  pharmacy windows.
- The Central Medical Service
  (☎ 5923434) can refer you to a duty
  GP or dentist.
- Hospital outpatient clinics are
  open 24 hours a day. The most
  central is Onze-Lieve-Vrouwe
  Gasthuis ✉ 's Gravesandeplein 16
  ☎ 5999111 🚊 Trams 3, 10, 17

Precautions

- Pickpockets are common in busy shopping streets and markets, and in the Red-Light District. Take sensible precautions and remain on your guard at all times.
- At night, avoid poorly lit areas and keep to busy streets. Amsterdam is not dangerous, but muggings do occur.
- There are no particular risks to women travelling alone. Wearing a wedding ring can help deter unwanted attention.

LANGUAGE

Basics

yes	ja
no	nee
please	alstublieft
thank you	bedankt
hello	hallo
good morning	goedemorgen
good afternoon	goedemiddag
good evening	goedenavond
good night	welterusten
goodbye	dag

Useful words

good/bad	goed/slecht
big/small	groot/klein
hot/cold	warm/koud
new/old	nieuw/oud
open/closed	open/gesloten
entrance/exit	ingang/uitgang
men's/women's lavatory	heren/damen wc
free/occupied	vrij/bezet
far/near	ver/dichtbij
left/right	links/rechts
straight ahead	rechtdoor

Restaurant

breakfast	het ontbijt
lunch	de lunch
dinner	het diner
menu	de kaart
winelist	de wijnkaart
main course	het hoofdgerecht
dessert	het nagerecht
the bill, please	mag ik afrekenen

Numbers

1	een	14	veertien
2	twee	15	vijftien
3	drie	16	zestien
4	vier	17	zeventien
5	vijf	18	achttien
6	zes	19	negentien
7	zeven	20	twintig
8	acht	30	dertig
9	negen	40	veertig
10	tien	50	vijftig
11	elf	100	honderd
12	twaalf	1,000	duizend
13	dertien		

Days and times

Sunday	Zondag
Monday	Maandag
Tuesday	Dinsdag
Wednesday	Woensdag
Thursday	Donderdag
Friday	Vrijdag
Saturday	Zaterdag
today	vandaag
yesterday	gisteren
tomorrow	morgen

Useful phrases

Do you speak English? Spreekt u engels?

Do you have a vacant room? Zijn er nog kamers vrij?

with bath/shower met bad/douche

I don't understand Ik versta u niet

Where is/are ..? Waar is/zijn?

How far is it to ..? Hoe ver is het naar?

How much does this cost? Hoeveel kost dit? …

What time do you open? Hoe laat gaat u open?

What time do you close? Hoe laat gaat u dicht?

Can you help me? Kunt u mij helpen?

Index

Top 25
Amsterdam

ABOUT THE AUTHOR

Teresa Fisher is a freelance travel writer and photographer who, having lived in mainland Europe for many years, remains a frequent visitor to Holland and, in particular, Amsterdam. She contributes regularly to a variety of newspapers and magazines at home and abroad and is the author of several AA publications including *Essential Provence*, *Spiral Paris* and *Spiral Florence* and, in this series, *CityPack Munich*.

EDITION REVISER George McDonald **CONTRIBUTIONS TO LIVING AMSTERDAM** Christopher Catling
MANAGING EDITORS Apostrophe S Limited
COVER DESIGN Tigist Getachew, Fabrizio La Rocca

A CIP catalogue record for this book is available from the British Library.

ISBN-10: 0 7495 5037 6
ISBN-13: 978 0 7495 5037 0

The contents of this publication are believed correct at the time of printing. Nevertheless, the publishers cannot be held responsible for any errors or omissions or for changes in the details given in this guide or for the consequences of any reliance on the information provided by the same. This does not affect your statutory rights. Assessments of attractions, hotels, restaurants and so forth are based upon the author's own personal experience and, therefore, descriptions given in this guide necessarily contain an element of subjective opinion which may not reflect the publishers' opinion or dictate a reader's own experiences on another occasion. We have tried to ensure accuracy in this guide, but things do change and we would be grateful if readers would advise us of any inaccuracies they may encounter.

Published by AA Publishing, a trading name of Automobile Association Developments Limited, whose registered office is Fanum House, Basing View, Basingstoke, Hampshire RG21 4EA. Registered number 1878835.

First published 1997. Reprinted Jan, Mar, Oct, Dec 1998, Mar 1999
Second edition 1999. Reprinted Oct 2000
Revised third edition 2002. Reprinted Oct 2002
Reprinted Feb 2003. Revised fourth edition 2004. Reprinted 2004
Information verified and updated 2005. Reprinted Feb 2006. Reprinted Jun 2006.

Colour separation by Keenes, Andover
Printed and bound by Hang Tai D&P Limited, Hong Kong

ACKNOWLEDGEMENTS

Teresa Fisher wishes to thank the Netherlands Board of Tourism, the VVV, British Midland, KLM UK, Hotel Maas, Hotel Nova, Damstraat Rent-a-Bike and Bikes-a-Gogo for their assistance in preparing this book. The Automobile Association wishes to thank the following photographers, libraries and museums for their assistance in the preparation of this book. AKG LONDON 16r, 17l, 17r; ANNE FRANKHUIS 33t; ARCAID 1 (Richard Bryant); BRIDGEMAN ART LIBRARY LONDON 16/17 Still life of shells with the Feast of the Gods c. 1615 (oil on copper) by Frans the Younger Francken (1581-1642) Johnny van Haeften Gallery, London UK; MARY EVANS PICTURE LIBRARY 40b; Museum Het Rembrandthuis 46t, 46b; ROBERT HARDING PICTURE LIBRARY 1b, 12r, 19b, 24r; HULTON GETTY 16l; MUSEUM WILLET-HOLYHUYSEN 45; EDDY POSTHUMA DE BOER 33b, 41, 48; RIJKSMUSEUM 28; SPECTRUM COLOUR LIBRARY 47; STOCKBYTE 5; VAN GOGH MUSEUM 27t, 27b; WOONBOOTMUSEUM 30; ZEFA PICTURES 52, 53. The remaining photographs are held in the Association's own library (AA PHOTO LIBRARY) and were taken by KEN PATERSON with the exception of the following: MAX JOURDAN 1t, 2, 4, 6, 8l, 8br, 9cr, 9bl, 10l, 10r, 10/1, 11tr, 11c, 12l, 13t, 13, 13r, 14l, 14r, 14/5, 15tl, 15tr, 18t, 18l, 18r, 19t, 19c, 20t, 20l, 21l, 22tl, 24tl, 51b; ALEX KOUPRIANOFF All front and back cover, 9cl, 9, 11tl, 20tc, 20tr, 21tl, 21r, 23tl, 24tr, 24l; WYN VOYSEY 22tr

A03091

TITLES IN THE TOP 25 SERIES

• Amsterdam • Barcelona • Berlin • Brussels & Bruges • Dublin • New York • Paris • Prague • • Rome • Venice •